Ghosts, Demons and Dolls

Erica Gammon

Raven Crest Books

Published by: Raven Crest Books
www.ravencrestbooks.com

Copyright © 2015 Erica Gammon

The right of Erica Gammon to be identified as the author of this work has been asserted by her in accordance with the Copyright, Designs and Patents Act 1988

All rights reserved.

Some names and identifying details have been changed to protect the privacy of individuals.

No part of this publication may be reproduced, stored in a retrieval system or transmitted in any form or by any means including photocopying, electronic, recording or otherwise, without the prior written permission of the rights holder, application for which must be made through the publisher.

ISBN-13: 978-0-9933747-8-4
ISBN-10: 0-99-337478-6

FOREWORD

Writing a Foreword to Erica's book has been an easy task, primarily because I thoroughly enjoyed reading it. Ghost stories and tales of the paranormal have a huge following and this collection of stories will definitely not disappoint, especially as they are true stories garnered from the author herself, and from several professional investigation groups.

Those that know me are aware that I have a phobia of dolls and the story about the raggedy doll, Genevieve, certainly pushed that button. Other stories range from haunted castles, railway stations and an underground bunker at an RAF base in Yorkshire, England. Phantom children's voices at play and a child holding the hand of someone who wasn't actually there, will bring on the shivers and reading with the light on is recommended.

What makes this collection of stories stand out is the fact that they are accurate accounts of personal experiences. They are told with a genuine interest in the paranormal and without unnecessary embellishment, all of which highlights the scary nature of the events as they unfold.

Erica's first book will appeal to all who have an interest in the paranormal and the downright creepy and bring a satisfactory shiver down the spine.

Jan McDonald
Author of the 'Mike Travis Paranormal Investigations' series

INTRODUCTION

Well, firstly I must thank you if you are reading this as it means you have spent your well-earned money on my book. I have to tell you that I have been thinking of writing this for some years and only now have I decided that the time feels right to do it. It is a very scary prospect, putting words on paper (or some electronic device), for the whole world to read, at least I hope that some of you will take the time to read it.

This book is going to tell you ghost stories which none of you will ever have read before, that is because they happened to me and friends and others who also contributed their experiences, and most of all they are all true. I also promised I would not name anyone without their permission to do so, so if they are not named you know why this is.

There seems to be a plethora of TV shows covering this topic and I must admit, because of my experiences, I am quite addicted. Some I believe, some I do not. But you can rest assured that the stories I shall tell here have never been written in book form before. They may not all be scary, hide-behind-the-sofa tales, but I hope that they make you have a little shiver. There is, in my opinion, more than this one life, although I'm not sure what form that it takes – you may not agree with me, but I shall leave that decision up to you.

I have been one of the people in life that have not had to go looking for ghosts and ghostly occurrences – they seem to come to me. I am still not sure if this is a good thing or not. I have found that, looking back over the stories here, not all scary stories have to have ghosts, demons' or other entities in them to be downright worrying! I have never been on a ghost hunt either, but that may change in the future, it all depends on how brave (or stupid some may say) I am feeling at the time.

So, I thank everyone who has contributed to this book, my husband Roger who kept urging me to get on and do it and of course those people from Twitter who had the experiences and took the time to write them down and send them to me. I have written them exactly as they have been given; I feel it is not up to me to alter them in any way, after all, the experiences were not all mine and I wasn't there. So, what you read is as it happened and I hope you enjoy them. I must admit, I thought at the beginning that this was going to be very easy to put together, but to get the stories here has been somewhat of a struggle. It seems to me not everyone is comfortable to share what happened to them, which is understandable. A lot of people still don't believe, even though the evidence is plain to see, hear, feel, or even smell in some cases!

I also need to thank all my followers on social media – (Twitter!) – I couldn't have done this without you guys (and girls of course!) and I also thank you for putting up with my pleas to try to get the stories in; you have been badgered, berated and cajoled more times than I can count! All for your pleasure my dear reader(s) – the things we do to try and please!

THE HOUSE IN CASTLE ROAD

My brother was born in November when I was about four years old, and my parents decided to buy a house in Saltwood as the one they rented was in a very bad state and was very small. In fact it was almost falling down – the only thing keeping the walls up was the roof. They bought a house in Castle Road opposite Saltwood Castle. It had previously been owned by an old lady called Miss Mowl (I love that name!) who had died sometime before in a nursing home.

The house was an end of terrace and had three bedrooms and a long back garden and at the top there were two very big apple trees. I don't think we could have been there very long. Mum said to me, when she told me this story a long time later, that she had been lying in bed one night with the curtains open and looking toward the bottom of the bed, when she realised there was an old lady with long white hair in a nightdress with a shawl around her shoulders standing with her arms crossed, watching my father and her sleep. I asked if she was scared and mum said that she wasn't and she felt quite peaceful, somehow she knew it was Miss Mowl who she felt had just come back to check on the new people who had bought her house, then she said she just rolled over and went to sleep. She also said she knew she was a ghost as she could see the apple trees through her! I think my mum was also someone who had more experiences than she let on about, or she would have been more spooked by that happening than she was. Maybe I inherited my "intuitions" from her. I also think that it may have run in the family, as you will see later. I have also just remembered that after we had been there only a short while, my parents got the house blessed by our local Vicar, Eric Stanton. He was a Church of England minister and I don't know if this was usual in those days. Maybe there had been activity already?

GRANDMA'S HOUSE – PART ONE

I was born in a little village called Saltwood in Kent, in the front bedroom of my grandmother's house. I am very lucky to be here at all as it was not an easy birth for my mother – in fact I nearly died as the cord was wrapped around my neck. But, as you can tell, I am here and writing all that happened to me over the years in the little village where I spent a lot of my life.

I won't give you the number of the house or the street name as the house is still there and occupied but, you never know, the same may be happening to the occupants even now. If they read this and it strikes a chord, please feel free to let me know!

The first time I realized that something was a bit odd in that house was when I was about sixteen. I had moved away from the village as my parents had decided to take a pub in the Medway Towns, but I used to go back at every opportunity to see Gran and have the weekend with my best friend Jinny. The things we got up to were something else; the terrible twins we certainly were (and if given half the chance we still would be)! One night I had been out with Jinny and we had been fooling around as usual and as it was very late I went off back to Gran's house. It was an awful place to get to the back door, especially at gone one in the morning. You walked up the road and then turned into a short alley that ran between two houses then had to go through the neighbour's back yard before turning into my grandmother's yard and finally got to the back door. There were no lights in the back gardens and everything was completely black. I always hurried as I have been blessed (or sometimes I think cursed!) with a very active imagination and every time I went up the alley I was expecting to turn the corner and find someone or, even worse, something, waiting for me as I walked through. Of course there never was.

The house was of the Victorian style, and when I was a small girl it still had a toilet outside and the house had gas lamps. There was no bathroom either and everyone had to wash in the kitchen sink. It was good that there was a very high fence blocking the view from the neighbour's kitchen, otherwise it would have been very embarrassing! The only problem with that was that at night, if you were in the kitchen, you felt like you were being watched and if you turned around there might be a face looking in the window at you. I am sure some of you know what that feels like – quite disconcerting and very creepy!

Well, things had been considerably modernised by the time I was sixteen; the house had 'all mod cons' and hot water and electric lights and even an indoor bathroom. Very modern, my grandmother thought. She was quite old-fashioned. She called the kitchen "the scullery", the dining room was just that and was also the main room where she and my grandfather mainly lived. They each had their own cottage-style armchair either side of the fire, and I mention this as I have more to tell you about that later! Off the dining room was the door to the very steep flight of stairs which led to two bedrooms, one at the front and my grandparent's room at the back. Past the stairs was the front room, which was hardly ever used and saved for "best". The bedroom at the front was mine when I stayed and looked out onto the road. Thank goodness there were street lights there. As you walked into the room on the left wall was a small fireplace, then in the recess next to it a tall chest of drawers. The wall facing the road had two sash windows and, in between them, a dressing table which had a three-part mirror and four drawers. The wall that adjoined next door on the right had a large wardrobe with a full-length mirror on the door and a drawer below. The wall where the large bed was placed also had a small cupboard with a shelf in, and locked by way of a latch. The big bed was the one I was born in and the mattress was a lumpy feather one and when you got in to it, you just automatically rolled into the middle and it cocooned you so that you had to fight your way uphill to the edge when it was time to get up. I have never slept in one so comfortable since.

I have gone into a lot of detail about what the room contained as it is around this furniture my story starts. I lay in bed that night when I got in and was thinking about what little devils Jinny and I were; not in a bad way, now I think back, but in silly ways. I loved visiting what I still considered my home, even though I had moved away three years before. Saltwood was and always will be home to me.

It was while I was lying there, nowhere near falling asleep, that I heard a noise. At first I thought I was hearing things, but one of the drawers in the chest of drawers by the fire had opened; I heard it being ruffled through as if someone was looking for something, then pushed shut hard enough to make the handles rattle. I was not facing them at the time and thought it must be one of my grandparents, so I pretended to be sleeping – I didn't want them to know I had only been in about ten minutes! Then the next drawer down did the same, and the one after.

Every drawer in all the pieces of furniture in the room had the same thing happen, and by the time it got to the wardrobe, which I was facing, I had my eyes squeezed tightly shut; I didn't want to see who it was, as apart from the noise of the drawers there was not another sound. No breathing, no muttering, just nothing. I finally dropped off to sleep after it seemed liked I had lain there for hours, too scared to move.

I got up in the morning and got dressed and, as I did, I looked over at the drawers and I got a shock! You see, the handles which had rattled so loudly simply couldn't have: they were solid wood.

I thought things through and went downstairs and asked my grandparents if either of them had been going through drawers in their room last night? Both said no, and asked why? I told them the truth, but felt stupid as I did so. Then I got another shock – my grandmother said that a few months previously, my uncle and his new wife had stayed there, and they had heard exactly the same thing. I found out later that when my grandfather had been working for a removals company, they had picked up this set of furniture from a house and been asked to dispose of it, and my grandfather had bought it. So, who knows what had happened to it before? I just know I have never, and never will, buy second-hand furniture from anywhere.

GRANDMA'S HOUSE – PART TWO

I have to say, that experience in the front bedroom of that house did happen again – and more than once, but it didn't worry me so much after the first time. Yes, it was scary, but nothing ever came near the bed (that I know of!) and I kept my eyes tightly closed and put my fingers in my ears when it started. I was never tempted to peek and see what was happening or who was doing it; I felt safer not knowing.

I was visiting again and had had a great weekend with my friend Jinny. I was by then in my late teens and we had been clubbing on the Friday and Saturday nights and had both had a whale of a time as we always did. I can't say that I remembered anything strange on either of those nights when I got home, except the awful feeling that I might find someone waiting in the garden or following me as I made my way up the passage between the houses. That happened every time I went back late at night, or even early in the mornings!

This time it was a bright, sunny Sunday morning and I was just at the top of the stairs and about to go in to the front bedroom. I stopped and looked at the step into the bedroom as there was a shadow on it I couldn't quite believe was there. I was looking at what seemed to be a shadow of a pair of hanging legs, just from the knees down. The shadow appeared to be of someone hanging down from the bedroom door jamb. This time I ran back down and made my grandmother come back with me; I had to show her and make sure it wasn't just me who could see them. We got back to the top and I went into the bedroom and she stayed on the small landing and looked in, and I showed her what I saw.

She saw them too, but it didn't seem to concern her at all! I had to ask her again and pointed out the shadow and she again confirmed she saw them. I asked her what they could be doing there; had anyone hanged themselves in the house before she took it over? I was stunned by her reply: no one had hung themselves in this house but there had been a man over the road who had, but that was years ago, she said! She wasn't in the least worried about seeing them, not like me. I was stunned. I have a funny feeling now, looking back on these things that happened. I think she might have seen and heard more than she liked to let on. My grandfather wouldn't have believed her if she had told him. He wouldn't believe anything he couldn't see with his own eyes, and would have told her to stop imagining things.

There are a couple of other things I have to tell you about that happened in that house. I had been married for about six months and my new husband and I had bought a house in Lydd. As we had a few days to kill before we could move in, we decided to go and stay at my grandmother's and he could also use the time to go and see his mother, who lived in Dymchurch. We had been there a few nights and nothing spooky had happened and I had not mentioned anything that had happened previously when I stayed there. Then the morning before we moved into our new house, my husband asked if I had slept well and I said of course, I always found that bed really great for sleeping in. I asked him why – hadn't he slept well? Again, we had the front bedroom.

He was on the side of the bed next to the cupboard in the wall, and he told me he had just been lying there and the door to the cupboard opened and a woman in a long white nightdress and long white hair almost to her waist had come out and walked straight through the bed and out of the door! I was shocked to say the least; I had never experienced this or anything like it and, what's more, the door to the cupboard was still shut when I looked over! I had felt absolutely nothing during the night. He decided there and then he would not be staying at Grandma's again, and never did. We never mentioned this to her, but my guess is she probably knew about it anyway. She had lived there so long that these things probably didn't worry her any more, and if they did she didn't bother talking to my grandfather about them, or anyone else that I know of.

GRANDMOTHER'S HOUSE – LAST PART

In my early twenties my parents took a public house in Swindon. I had some problems to sort out and decided that I would go back to stay in Saltwood for a while until I got things straight, and also to help my grandmother who was on her own, as my grandfather had died from throat cancer shortly before. He and my grandmother were smokers; he more so than her.

I had managed to get a job in a local hotel as a waitress on the breakfast and lunch shifts, but it did mean I had to be up around 5.30 am to get there for 7.00am as I had no car and had to get the bus.

One morning I was making a coffee in the kitchen and had only been up a short while. I was just putting my make-up on in the kitchen mirror when I distinctly heard the chair where my grandfather sat make a creaking noise as if someone had just sat down. Then there was a noise like someone clearing their throat. I thought it might have been my grandmother getting up early as she had possibly heard the kettle boiling, but the sound had definitely been a man. I looked into the dining room and saw there was no one there. Good morning, Grandad!

LYDD HOUSE

We moved into the house in Lydd, again I will not give you an address except to let you know it was near the green which the locals called "the Rype". Again, it was an old house and had previously been owned by a very old lady and her son. As far as I remember, she was in her nineties when she died and had lived with her son in the same house all her married life. The house only had one electric socket in the whole place and that was in the kitchen. This room had been well used: there was a concrete floor in it and, where the sink was, there was a dip where the old soul had stood for so many years. The kitchen was painted in lettuce-coloured green gloss paint and a real pain to get off the walls. The banisters which went up the stairs to the bathroom and two bedrooms we thought were painted black, but it was polish and dirt where hands had used them for so many years and not been cleaned back to the wood in all that time. To say we had a lot of work to do was an understatement.

By the end of six months of hard labour the house was looking good and feeling like home. It was about this time when we sat watching television in the late evenings that the letterbox started to bang loudly. Not like it would bang if someone was knocking to come in, just one very loud bang as if something had been posted through, although there was never any sound of anything landing on the carpeted floor. We used to go and check, and thought at first it must be the wind catching the flap, but it wasn't that as the flap was one that had a spring to stop that from happening. So we thought it was kids doing "ring and run", but we could never see anyone in the street when we checked; we even looked into the porches of the neighbours' houses but we never found a soul. In the end, after it had happened so often, we just put it down to one of the odd things that some houses do.

It wasn't too long after the letterbox started banging that I found I didn't much like going upstairs to our bedroom, which was at the front of the house. I didn't like the turn at the top of the stairs which led past the spare room (which still had floor boards up and junk all over it, as Hubby was re-wiring).

One day Hubby was at work and I went upstairs for something and behind me, as I got to the top of the stairs, I heard a stair creak, as one of them did and we had not got round to fixing yet. By this time I was past the spare room door and almost to our bedroom, the door of which was open and filled with sun. I looked back and was horrified to see, coming along the landing towards me, a shadow of a man in an old Forties-style brown pinstriped suit, the type with turn-up cuffs at the bottom of the trousers. It had a double-breasted jacket and a small pocket on the breast, but the wearer was just a shadow. I ran. The shadow man was no more than four feet away from me! I have never moved so fast in my life. I slammed the door behind me and jumped across the bed and hid behind the bottom corner; I was sobbing and trying not to make a noise, at the same time peeping up to see if the door opened. I stayed there for what felt like an hour or more, but really it could have been no more than two or three minutes. I had my eyes riveted to the door all the time waiting for the suited man to come in – and nothing did. After I had stopped crying I had to screw up all my courage and go back downstairs. I crept back to the bedroom door, trying not to make a sound, and it took so much effort to open the door as I was so scared but I did, little bit by little bit, and then suddenly pulled it all the way open – and there was nothing there. Crying again, I ran down the stairs and out the front door to my neighbour, Sue. I banged on her door so hard she opened it within seconds. I went in and she made me a cup of tea, and I felt really stupid when I told her what had happened. I don't think she believed me, but she could see what a state I was in. When the time came that I had to go home, she came in with me and checked the whole house and assured me there was no one there. She was still there when Hubby came back from work. I'm so grateful to her, so, Sue, if you remember, thank you again. I couldn't have gone in again if you hadn't been there.

I don't know about you, reader, but I have given this subject a lot of thought and it seems to me that some people just seem to attract "happenings", for want of a better word, more so than most of the population. This I think may have something to do with family; you may be able to "inherit" (again for want of a better word) the ability to have this type of experience. I don't know, of course, but if perhaps someone other than me had moved to that house in Lydd, would they have had the same things happen to them? A puzzling question, but not one I feel would benefit investigation by me. I am here only to put into words these "happenings". I shall leave it to someone far more qualified (and braver) than me to discover, if that is at all possible. Ghost hunting – from my perspective – is best left to being watched on television from the safety of the sofa, with a hot cup of coffee and the light on and, of course, the curtains closed! But I might be persuaded to go on one – one day.

I only have one more story for you that really happened to me (I heard that sigh of relief from here!) then I promise I shall go on to some stories that are far more interesting than mine.

THE SOUTH EASTERN – TONBRIDGE

I think that you may be aware from the heading for this story that it happened in a public house, and you would be correct. This was a pub that my parents had taken and I feel it would be safe to name it in this story as it is no longer a pub and may even not be there at all now. I know it closed as a pub and turned into a café, but from there, I don't know.

I do know that it was built when the railway was being built; that it had a cellar and, on the ground floor, there were two bars, a games room and at the back of the building, on the same floor, a kitchen and living room. The first floor had four bedrooms, a bathroom and a small toilet under the stairs. The stairs led up to a further three, I think, rooms at the top of the house. It may have been four, but the top floor was never used as there was no fire certificate available and it could not be used for letting bedrooms as it had been way back in the past.

The top floor was always dark even during the day and, again, was one of those places you just didn't look up at, in case you saw someone looking over the banister back at you. I got the creeps every time when I was going past the bottom of the stairs up to that floor, so I usually ran past!

I had moved back in with mum and dad and my brother when my marriage broke down, and I worked for them in the bar. It was a busy pub and every evening always bustling with early commuters going home, and then the customers who just wanted a pint or two and some company. At the end of the day, dad meticulously cleaned all the ashtrays and cleaned the bar and washed all the glasses. This meant that he only had to re-stock the bar in the morning and, of course, give it a good clean.

It was only a few days after they moved in that the customers started to ask if he had met "our ghost" yet. He laughed and told them not to talk nonsense; there was no such thing. After a week or two, he changed his mind on that. As I said, he was very thorough on cleaning glasses and ashtrays before leaving the bar at night. You had to be very mindful that nothing caught fire and there was nothing worse than having to wash the glasses and smelly ashtrays in the mornings. However, on a few occasions, in the morning, he went to let the cleaner in – and he found three or four used glasses on the bar. He knew for certain they had all been cleaned and put away the previous evening. Hmmm, strange! Especially when the cleaner said that often happened.

The pub, as I have mentioned, was built when the railway was being built, and the customers all said that it was a place where "loose ladies", as they put it, entertained the workers at the end of their shifts. It was a huge place inside, with so many bedrooms, that this was entirely feasible. This was years ago, but the thing is: one of the ladies had seemed to like the place so much she stayed behind. Quite often, if you were going upstairs, there would be a waft of Attar of Roses perfume come past you. You never saw her; just smelled the perfume. The whole of the family had smelt it at one point or another. I remember one day, sitting in the living room with my mother, and she said, "I have a visitor over here. Go and stand by Erica, your perfume is too strong for me." And she did. She must have been standing right next to me, but it wasn't in the least scary. No cold spots, just her perfume. I have no idea why I wasn't scared, but it just didn't worry me in the least. I suppose we had all got used to smelling the perfume in various different places so often it didn't seem to worry any of us. She wasn't threatening in any way, we all seemed to just accept the fact she was there. After all, she was there a long time before we were.

My grandfather was a Geordie (from Newcastle) and,

as I said before, wouldn't believe anything he couldn't see. He had a heart attack while we had the South Eastern and came to us for a week or two for recuperation, without my grandmother. Dad brought him back and he was having a cup of tea while dad took his case up, and telling mum about what had happened. Then, after the tea, he went up to unpack. A little while later, mum went up to see if he needed a hand. As she went in the room he asked, "Have you spilled a bottle of perfume in here? It stinks." Mum told him about the lady, but he wouldn't believe her. There is just no convincing some people, even when the proof is right under your nose.

THE FARMER'S STORY

As a small boy, my husband, Roger, lived on a farm near Folkestone in Kent with his father.

The farm is on a very high hill and is still in Roger's family – it is now run by his brother. The fields around are full of rabbits, foxes and badgers. I love going to the farm as it is bordered by woods and the scenic views are spectacular; you can see for miles. The nearest neighbour is about a mile away. It is a nature lover's dream. Being in such a secluded place, it was not uncommon for back doors to be left open back then; there was never anyone brave enough to try and steal anything as there were dogs who would bark furiously and alert their owner to a stranger's presence – besides which, most farmers had guns to hand in those days, and more often than not they were loaded.

The farm did, however, have one problem and that was poachers. Most of them were chased off by Roger's father, but there was one group who were not to be messed with on any account, as Roger's father told him. They were really unsavoury characters and best avoided at all costs. Roger was quite young at the time and used to go wandering around the farm in the middle of the night if he could not sleep. The farm was also used by the army for training purposes, and Roger liked to try and get into their camps without being noticed.

On the occasion in question, it must have been very early in the morning and everyone in the house was asleep, when the dogs started barking furiously, waking Roger and his father instantly. They both rushed downstairs as the kitchen door burst open. The group of men who flew into the kitchen were the poachers Roger had been warned about. They were in quite a state and very breathless, and frightened out of their wits.

When Roger's father asked them what the hell was going on, one of the men told him that they had been setting their nets across the rabbit holes, as they had put ferrets down the holes to flush the rabbits out. They were sitting waiting for their ferrets to appear from the holes when they saw a light coming down the slope of the bank: it was a man with an old-fashioned lamp walking down towards them. They challenged him and asked what the f... he thought he was doing? The man answered them, saying, "I have walked these hills for centuries longer than you".

Without waiting they dropped everything right where it was and sprinted back to the farm, which was about half a mile or so away, and they refused to leave until it was daylight. They never went back for their nets, rabbits or ferrets and they never went near the farm to poach again.

There was one other very short story my husband told me about. His father had a worker who lived in the small village at the bottom of the hill which was about two miles away, and the quickest way for him to get to work every morning was to go up the hill and cross the fields. This was always very early in the morning and normally, apart from the summer time, it was nearly always dark.

He happened to mention to them that every morning in the field nearest the farm's yard he saw someone with a light cutting diagonally past him near the fence line. No matter how hard he tried, he could never catch them up to see who it was. Well, winter time came around and the snow came down overnight and still the farm worker saw the light that morning. He thought that this time he would be able to catch up with him and see who it was. He hurried up a bit and still he couldn't catch up with whoever had the light. Strangest of all – there were no footprints in the snow to show any one had been there in the first place!

The next stories are ones that I have been given by generous Paranormal Societies and members of the general public. I can't thank them enough for the time they have taken in sending these to me. I am writing them just as they were given and have made no changes in the text. So, here we go, sit tight and make sure you have a light on! You may also want to check all the doors and windows are locked before you start to read them. Close the curtains too, just in case.

This story is from Christine Donnelly of the Hidden Realms Paranormal group, who supplied this account of the night they went on an investigation to Torre Abbey in Torquay, England. She tells me:

Whilst we were collecting evidence of alleged hauntings, a member of the staff related this strange tale to us.

A family was visiting the building and in particular the room dedicated to Agatha Christie. Being big fans of hers they wanted to have a look at the items which had once belonged to her. The family group consisted of mum, dad, their young daughter and the grandmother. The CCTV filmed the group as they made their way around the exhibition. Unfortunately the little girl began to get bored and wander around the room by herself. She then made her way to the door and left the room, unseen by the rest of the family. She raised her hand in the air and took hold of what she thought was her grandmother's hand. She then happily walked along the corridor into another part of the Abbey, still holding the hand. In the chapel area she let go of the hand and turned, hoping to see her grandmother but there was nobody there. She became very distressed and started to cry. Luckily, a visitor found her and took her to a member of staff, who could see that she was very upset as she couldn't find her grandmother. The Staff member remembered seeing the little girl with her family in the Agatha Christie exhibition room and took her back to them. When they reached the room, the little girl saw her grandmother there and ran to her and asked her why she had left her alone. The grandmother was puzzled as she had been with the child's parents all the time and had never left the room. This begged the question – whose hand had the little girl been holding?

The staff and family were quite concerned about this in case there was a child abductor in the building, and went to see the CCTV footage on the TV to see if they could find out who had been holding the child's hand. They wound it back and saw all the family together in the Agatha Christie room, they then saw the little girl smile as she raised her hand and begin to walk along the corridor as if she was holding onto something. The camera filmed her walking through the Abbey and into the chapel area where she was seen to become distressed, with her hand back down by her side. Was it a friendly spirit who wished the child no harm and just wanted to take her for a little walk? Unfortunately we will never know, as since this happened the CCTV footage has been recorded over by the Abbey staff.

This next tale is from Dennis Hemmings, who is also a member of Hidden Realms Paranormal group. This is a story which has been covered by the British TV programme 'Most Haunted', but Dennis has sent it to me to be told as it happened in his own words.

WEST RAYNHAM AIRFORCE BASE, NORFOLK, ENGLAND

I enlisted in the RAF for my National Service in 1952. I attended training for medical work for three months and was eventually posted to RAF West Raynham in Norfolk, as part of the staff in the station sick-quarters/hospital. There were duty shifts of one ambulance crash driver, and two medical staff. The shift stayed in the building while there was active flying and remained in a dedicated room with a crash alarm and a grid map of the surrounding area. The ambulance crash driver always remained in the building on the ground floor with a duplicate alarm and map.

Our particular room was on the first floor off a short corridor which led to a room for twenty patients, but there were none occupying the beds that night. My colleague was Colin Bragger. Colin was a docker by profession and although he appeared to begrudge his National Service stint, his formidable size and no-nonsense attitude belied his really good nature.

The ground floor housed the administration, doctors and pharmacy during the daytime, but the whole building had to be left illuminated in case any outside staff or families needed help after hours.

Around 11.30 pm we received a call from the control tower telling us we could stand down as the last aircraft had landed. We had two beds which were separated by a table with a telephone. We got undressed and got into bed. I couldn't have been asleep very long when I was woken abruptly by the bed clothes being dragged off of me. My immediate reaction was to get out of bed and return what I thought was an ill-timed prank by pulling the bedding off Colin. My colleague awoke and was extremely angry at my action; had it not been for a loud and distracting noise outside the door, I am sure it would not have ended there.

The door had a clear glass window and through it we could see a dark, smoke-like cloud in the well-illuminated corridor. The noise was best described as like two wooden wardrobes being violently smashed and splintering together in mid-air. The cloud and noise came from a source which was only about five feet in front of us and we both were terrified. Colin was ashen, as I am sure I was. There was not a lot that could scare us easily with a physical presence, but there was no physical source. The whole disturbance seemed to last an eternity but in retrospect it was only about fifteen to twenty seconds.

Our first move was to phone the RAF Police; it seemed rather lame but we said we thought we had an intruder. The police turned up with a guard dog and we had to let them in the main door. The dog refused to go up the stairs but both floors were searched by the police. The building was found to be secure. There were no stories or rumours about the place, but Colin and I made every excuse to avoid sleep-over duty there.

In the mid 60's we moved to Norfolk and met an ex-service man who had been a patient at West Raynham. He also complained he had had the bed clothes removed while he was the only patient in the ward, but there was no accompanying noise.

'Most Haunted' visited the airfield and buildings during a programme in 2010 but there were no unusual happenings during the part when they visited the station's sick quarters of the Hospital.

RAF West Raynham was turned into a missile unit and is now a housing development.

The next story is from Deedee Casey, who is part of the Paranormal Searchers and Investigators of Ireland. This is one of the first stories I received, and for that I thank her very much.

Deedee wrote to me and said that her very first paranormal experience happened when she was a child:

Me, my mum and dad used to live in a house in Spring Madden Court in West Belfast. Every night I used to wake up and the room would be icy cold and there would be a man and woman standing at the foot of my bed in old, raggy clothes. I will be honest and say it scared me as I thought there were burglars in the house, so I used to scream for my mum and dad to come into the room, but of course they couldn't see anything – or at least that is what they wanted me to believe. Upon asking my dad about it a few years ago, he told me there were spirits in the house as he and my mum experienced them, but he didn't want to tell me about it in case it scared me.

This next offering is one I received from Noe Oliver, who saw a request I had put on Twitter for stories. In parts it reads a little bit technical, but takes nothing away from the story. I said at the beginning: I am giving them to you as they were given to me.

SPIRIT RECOGNITION

I have worked in acute psychiatry for two decades now; I practice psychotherapy. The contextual setting of my practice is currently spent between two acute inpatient psychiatric hospitals. There is absolutely nothing anyone can tell me or show me that will surprise me or that I will ever doubt, as I have been afforded the opportunity to work with some of the most brilliant humans beings. In my downtime, one of my favourite hobbies is researching and delving deeper into the paranormal.

Approximately two weeks ago, I ventured into an old house up the hill and across the street from where I live. I have always felt an unsettled energy when walking or driving past this particular house, for nearly fourteen years now. It has been abandoned here on the hill for well over forty years. Like I said, approximately two weeks ago I went into the house by myself for an informal investigation. While in the house I snapped a few pictures, yet they came out completely black at the time. After I got home I discovered images in two of the photographs (pictures not supplied with story). I had my EVP and EMF meters with me and decided to use them. What I received through my EVP was a little boy by the name of "Mathew" who lived there along with his father "Philip" and his mother "Sonja". "Mathew" told me he died by choking on a sponge one morning when his mother and father were out back, gardening. "Mathew" went on to provide me with the words: ground, sponge, drowned, Mother, Father, sorry and regret. Of course at the time I felt all this to be quite peculiar, having nothing to connect these words with and not giving this experience another thought.

Thirteen days later I was conducting a standard psychiatric interview at one of hospitals I currently work at; since the beginning of my career as a psychotherapist I have administered thousands of these interviews. The patient's name (of course all names have been changed because of patient confidentiality) is Terri. Terri is a twenty-seven year old single female who has never been married and has just recently relocated here from Montana. Terri had a child out of wedlock while a sophomore at college; the child is in the custody of her parents. Terri describes her child as uncontrollable and difficult to manage.

This was Terri's first acute psychiatric admission. Terri's initial presenting problem to the emergency department was "gross internal disorganisation, inability to care for herself and walking in traffic". Terri was brought to the emergency department by the police department. Terri also has epilepsy and had reportedly had seven or eight grand mal seizures approximately forty-eight hours before being found walking in traffic.

My first thought after having gathered this information was that this was not a mental health crisis but rather a neurological crisis, nevertheless Terri was admitted directly from the emergency department to the inpatient acute psychiatric unit for observation and medical stabilisation.

During the interview Terri presented as quite foggy in effect. Flat and vacant, providing a flagrant difficulty in accessing information, as well as pulling information out of, and was presenting as quite the unreliable historian.

Both Terri's UDS (Urine Drug Screen) and blood work came back unremarkable which is an indication that none of her behaviour was drug-induced. I decided to come back the following day, given Terri's drastic recent change in mental status and inability to properly engage in a psychiatric interview.

The following day Terri presented remarkably clearer and medically stable with absolutely no recollection of the events that led to the police being called and being admitted to the emergency department for "bizarre behaviour in the community". We went through the standard intake questions, all of which were congruent with what the emergency department social worker was able to gather after having spoken to her parents in Montana.

Terri had suffered from epilepsy since she was eight. She is unable to work due to her epilepsy, yet takes care of a friend's (Terri's word) little boy from time to time for extra money to supplement her Social Security disability income. Toward the end of the interview I always ask the question about spiritual care and religious orientation. Terri went on to tell me she had been seeing a spiritual advisor/counsellor/friend who had the name of "Sonja" for the last seven years, and it was "Sonja's" son "Mathew" who Terri watches after to earn extra money.

The next stories I have for you are from Warren Coates who is a member of NIPRA which is the Northern Ireland Paranormal Research Association. These are based on a series of investigations at the Crumlin Road Gaol, in Belfast, Northern Ireland, which he and his team carried out over the space of a few months.

Wednesday 25th March

At 20.00 hours, Jo, Warren M, Michael, Simon and myself all set up equipment and got the feel of this amazing building. The first night was just to conduct a baseline test and get to know the natural noises heard. We were on site just over an hour when we all became aware of noises and a feeling which seemed to put everyone on edge; nothing more made itself known to us.

First we all became aware of lights moving along the walls of the wing, then we all heard the voice of a man calling out, nobody could make out what it was saying but it was a strong male voice. At just past midnight we packed up and left, knowing that the next time we went there we would investigate for real.

Tuesday 31st March

19.00 hours: the investigation starts. Warren M, Jo, Simon and myself set the camcorders and voice recorders up and all got ready for a good night. Sitting in the circle we started to call out and invite the spirit people to join us, but all was quiet. Moving down to the "drop cell" we again called out. After a while we all heard footsteps coming from above us and waited for someone to walk in and look over the safety rail at us, but nobody appeared.

So, Warren M and Jo went up to check all was clear. We knew the guards would be in their security hut, away from where we were. After a while we went down to the tunnel to see if we could get any activity down there. We went halfway down the tunnel and under the Crumlin Road where we felt a rush of icy cold air pushing by us. We all saw the figure of a man at the far end looking back at us – slowly he faded away and vanished before us.

We split up and a few of us went down to C wing; the rest including myself went to D wing.

No sooner had we all sat down and did a pathworking session, than we heard heavy breathing and noises coming from one of the cells. Both me and Warren M had got up to make our way over to investigate, when both of us saw a shadow come out of the cell and move very fast to the stairs and down to the second level. We went down but all was still, and after that the whole building went quiet so that at 2.00 am we called it a night and left.

Wednesday 1st April

20.00 hours. Members present: Warren M, Jo, Jarlath and myself. We had full run of the Gaol tonight, so made the most of it. We set voice recorders and camcorders in the tunnel; another voice recorder in the "drop cell". We all sat in B wing outside the padded cell.

After sitting around for half an hour we decided to do a séance. After only a short while we all felt the spirit energy coming down towards us as soon as we called out a name. As soon as we did this we all felt the rush of cold air circle us, we also heard a man sigh and a deep feeling of sadness. We also felt there were several energies trying to contact us. We were given names, which are now being checked to see if they are names known at the Gaol, and we won't make any of the names public yet until we get the results.

There were several bangs and the sound of something being dragged down the floor, but all we saw were the movements in shadows as they watched from a distance.

We at first thought it was going to be a quiet night but at 22.45 pm a loud bang was heard coming from the top of the stairs and the tunnel, and the sound of what we can only describe as the sound of a heavy table being moved from one side of the tunnel to the other, but when checked nothing had been moved. At 2.30 am we packed up and left. On checking our evidence we have several EVP's (electronic voice phenomenon), including the heavy bang we all heard, some strange things on digital camera and some video evidence, which we will upload at a later stage. Roll on next time.

Thursday 9th April
20.00 hours. Members present: Warren M, Jarlath and myself. We set up the equipment and took some photos with the UV lamp. We then went down to the "drop cell" and called out. After half an hour we all jumped when the door (a very heavy door leading from the execution room) slammed shut. It was a windy night out but still, this is a strange one. We then set the voice recorder down in the "drop cell" and went and sat in the flogging room with the door shut. We then invited spirits to join us and all of a sudden we were all made aware of a woman sitting down and sobbing in the corner (we all heard her moan and a woman's voice call out). There was also the spirit of one of the guards who stood outside the door; his breathing could be heard with a feeling of dislike (we all felt a bit uneasy with this energy).

After an hour we went up into D wing and again all felt uneasy with the feeling of being watched. As usual, D wing showed itself to be the most active part in the building with noises like walking, a strange clicking sound and several bright lights moving around the third level and three of us saw a man standing on the second level, leaning over and watching us.

Several photos were taken and video footage was also shot but nothing can be seen in it at all. The rest of the night was quiet but when reviewing the digital recorder in the "drop cell", we heard movement close to it along with breathing and a male grunt (at the time of recording this, we were in a distant room with the door closed). All in all, it was a very good night.

Thursday 7th May
19.00 hours. On several other occasions while at the Gaol we had very little activity (this is to be expected in investigations; not all the time do we see or hear things). We all arrived and set up the equipment, two members were in B wing and the other two, one being myself, were in D wing. At 20.45 there was a loud bang that came from the second floor (we were up on the third level). Thinking it was one of our members or one of the security staff we called out and asked if they needed a torch on, but getting no answer we went to investigate on the third floor landing. We were sure we saw a man walking into one of the cells and, thinking it was one of our team, we called out and went to see who it was. On getting to the door we were taken aback when we found the whole cell empty. On taking a reading we found it to be several degrees colder than the rest of the building. We radioed the other members and met up only to find that they had been having their own activity in B wing.

Thursday 14th May
19.00 hours. On getting to the Gaol we set the cameras up in B, C and D wings; also in the tunnel. The night seemed to start very quiet but at 21.35 we saw a light at the back of D wing. Both myself and Jo went to check this out, only to find the camcorder had been turned off and pushed down towards the floor. I called Warren M and Jarlath to go and check out the recorders; all was well except for one in the tunnel where the tripod was lying on the floor. We are very careful and make sure everything is set up and working before we leave the room, so this was very strange. After

re-setting the camcorders, we went up and sat in a group in D wing. We heard bangs, saw lights and heard heavy footsteps on the stairs, but on checking the equipment we had caught what sounded like breathing and footsteps.

The tapes belonging to the recorders which had strange things happen to them showed nothing; in fact, the one in the tunnel turned off while it was in the standing position. This was one very weird, strange night.

Thursday 21st May
19.00 hours. We had been lucky enough to have spoken to three warders who had worked in the Crumlin Gaol and they were not shocked when we told them about the activity we had happen to us in D wing. They told us that wardens and inmates alike hated D wing and a lot of people had experiences in it.

This night, we sat two members in D wing and a few in the circle. After settling down we heard a knocking sound coming from the direction of the tunnel but when we went to check on it we found nothing, but then heard knocking in the circle. We all felt we were being played with. At 22.00 hours we had started putting some equipment away when we heard an almighty bang coming from the chapel. We did not go up but we all saw lights, in other words orbs, flying out from the chapel and up towards D wing. This was an amazing thing to watch.

Thursday 4th June
19.00 hours. Well, this turned out to be one of the most amazing, scary and weird nights we have had in the Gaol. The night was quiet from 19.00 until 20.35 hours. We were in the basement in D wing and all were made aware of a deep feeling of depression and hatred. We split up into two groups of two; Jo and Warren M in the middle cell and myself in the bottom cell. Warren M called out to me and asked me if I had looked around the cell door, I replied no, I was sitting down on the stool in the cell. He

told me that both he and Jo had seen a young man around 21-years-old look round the right-hand side of the door (the strange thing was I saw a young man walk by my cell door towards them). Thinking it was a trick of the light I never told them, but I soon did after sitting watching people walk around the room and hearing whispers coming from the top of the wing. We knew time was getting on so we went to the circle to start putting things away – then all hell broke loose.

Myself and Jo were sitting on the wall by the spiral staircase; Warren M was standing in front of us chatting. We were all shut up by a door on the third floor slamming shut, then footsteps on the top landing. Warren M let out a shout, and looking up at him I saw he was pointing and looking up to the third floor where he had seen the full figure of a man dressed in a uniform walk along the top landing. Thinking there was nothing much more going to happen, we were proven wrong. Several of the team were walking down the basement in D wing getting equipment ready to put away. I saw what I first thought was a bag or blanket on the floor but leaning on the wall, as I got closer I was given the name – we shall call it Fred – and he had been stabbed to death by fellow inmates. He was crying and saying he had been killed in the wrong and was blamed for touching children. I was taken aback, as was the rest of the group; we had been given a full name and a reason why he had been killed (we later found out that a young man of this name was indeed killed in this area and by a knife and he was in for nothing to do with children but for theft). We were all a bit shaken by what had just happened so we began to make our way back up to the circle. It was like someone had lifted a heavy weight from us all. We all sat down and had a coffee, but even here we could all still hear the noises of things being moved and keys being turned. Then, soon as we started to make our way up the stairs everything went dead. After thirty five minutes we called it a night – but what a night!

Warren Coates was also good enough to send me this next offering about an investigation he and his team undertook in County Armagh, Northern Ireland.

RICHHILL CASTLE

Richhill (or Rich Hill) Castle is believed to have its origins around 1665 when built by Major Edward Richardson. The building is believed to be one of the first unfortified castles to be built in Ireland. The Castle was built on a hill by Richardson and was shortened to Richhill and gave its name to the town. NIPRA first got involved with it around 2004 when we were asked to do a four-part documentary for Radio Ulster with the late great Gerry Anderson. NIPRA was asked to conduct an investigation into this amazing building with some absolutely fantastic results, and below are just some of our results.

One night our group had set up full-spectrum cameras and tracking cameras around several locations around the Castle. Jarlath and myself were in the Death Room, Liz and Tanya were in the Séance Room, and Ian and Dawna were in the Hallway downstairs.

The first part of the night was quiet and the only sounds were the natural sounds of the building cooling down. Around 22.30pm Liz radioed me asking if we were walking around the floor; I replied 'no' as did the other group, but she could still hear footsteps. Then, both Jarlath and myself heard heavy footsteps coming up the stairs towards the Death Room. Thinking it was going to be Gordon, the Castle owner, calling in to see us, I called out that we were in the Death Room. The door leading from the landing into our room swung open fast, hitting the wall, but nobody was in the doorway. We went into the Hall to check but Jarlath and myself were instantly frozen – the whole corridor was plunged into icy coldness. This was a June evening and was quite warm outside. We all sat back down and called for spirits to join us and after about ten minutes both witnessed coloured lights float around the room and pass into an antique mirror in one corner of the room. The rest of the night passed with no further activty.

A few weeks later, we were all in the Death Room conducting a séance. After a short time calling to spirits, we all felt a drop in temperature and the feeling a spirit was in the room with us. One by one we all felt a tall man dressed in old military uniform walk around the circle and stop behind me. I felt him rest his hands on my shoulders and felt a deep sense of peace, then he moved away and did the same with three other members of our group. Later, on speaking to the owner, he told us that a few members of his family had seen or been aware of this man over the last fifty-four years. We go to a site with an open mind; we don't research the history of it but work with spirits to give the information. Later that night we were standing in the Upper Landing discussing the night when we all heard a woman saying "thank you" and watched as a bird's feather floated down and rested at our feet; this is usually regarded as a gift from the spirit world.

One of the most spectacular nights we had at the Castle was around February, a few years ago. It was a sad time as Gordon, the owner, had passed away at the end of the year and this was our first time back to the Castle. We sat for a good few hours with nothing much happening apart from the odd light floating around the room and noises of the house which seemed like the normal ones. Sitting in the kitchen/dining room at the big mahogany dinner table, we called out asking one of our friends from the spirit world to show. We were all drawn toward the corner of the room and were aware of what looked like a heat vapour rise, then the figure of a young woman materialized with long black hair, a white top and a skirt down to the floor. She smiled at us and slowly faded away. This was an amazing experience and was like finding the Holy Grail. We tried to contact her through a séance but with no joy. Later that night, while collecting our equipment from around the Castle we were amazed to find a camera had been turned round on its tripod to face the wall. Checking the footage you can see it turn around with a slow, jittery movement but nothing comes towards the camera even though we had it facing the door and the window. The Castle is closed now for a few years, getting renovation work, but we hope to get back to it when it reopens.

This next offering is also from Warren at NIPRA. It is with regard to a haunting in County Tyrone, Northern Ireland, that he and his team investigated on the 23rd November 2004. He says…

…after getting over ten emails and calls regarding the sighting of an old woman standing at the side of the road and watching people passing, then disappearing over a wall, through a bridge; and also another figure of a young woman walking in front of cars then disappearing, we were asked by a local resident to come down and do an investigation in the area to see if we could find anything.

The first night we went to investigate was the 26th November 2004. After meeting the resident we went to the places where the woman was seen. Brian set up a camcorder and Linda was using the digital voice recorder. We went up to the ruined house which was set back in the trees; we had two members there and two at the road.

After sitting for an hour (and getting some weird looks from passing traffic), I got the name " X " given to me and I could see an old woman across the road watching us. She was around seventy years of age with tied-up dark grey hair, and what struck me as not very happy looking. We sat on for another hour, but with nothing else happening we went home. Checking video tapes and recorders we found nothing out of the ordinary.

The second night of the investigation was on the 3rd December 2004. We got to the site and set the equipment up. After two hours we were all aware of a woman's voice and got an impression of sadness and anger. We were just getting ready to leave when myself and Brian saw the woman again looking at us. I walked to where we saw her and straight away felt overcome with sadness, to the extent that tears were running down my cheeks. The spirit told me she could not cross over until something to do with her land and the church had been rectified.

The third night we went down was the 15th December 2004, and we decided to focus on the house rather than on the road. Setting up the camcorders and EVP (electronic voice phenomenon) recorders, we sat down and started the vigil. We all soon became aware of the woman and also a man watching us. We tuned in and asked spirits to help us communicate with the spirit people present. We all felt a very deep sense of depression and that the house, the woman and the man needed help to move on. We did a clearing and all felt a more peaceful atmosphere around us. I know we have helped the spirit people here, but I don't think they will move on until the land thing has been sorted.

We visited the site again on the 23rd April 2005, and still feel the presence of the spirits in the area. We researched the area at the local library and found two cases of fatal accidents on the road and just up from the haunted site. We also found details of the old woman who lived in the house; we have been told she is the old lady who is haunting the road, but I am sure it is another spirit of a woman and not this one.

Update – 5th January 2009. Due to all the email, phone calls, TV and radio articles we have done over the past several weeks, we have revisited the site but, due to all the cars and sightseers trying to see the "lady in white", we have put off investigating until things settle down a bit. We did feel the spirit energy of an old woman; also a man who did not like to be seen, always moving away from us and staying in the shadows. We have spoken to several locals who will be helping us with our investigations and putting this case and its spirits to rest. So, keep watching for updates, the status of which is ongoing.

This next story is from Danielle Cahill. She sent her experience when she went on a ghost hunt with Warren and his team.

Famed for its ghostly apparitions, Ross Castle in County Meath is the sort of place where visitors can expect an encounter with all manner of things that go bump in the night. With that in mind, I spent a weekend with the Northern Ireland Paranormal Association (NIPRA), in search of the spirits who are said to haunt the rooms of this old country estate. The five-bedroomed stone castle was built in 1536 and is now run as a B&B by Benita and Sam Walker.

During weekends when NIPRA visits, the owners allow guests to have the run of the estate, although they do pop in to cook everyone breakfast and to see if there were any paranormal encounters the previous night!

I have never seen a ghost or had a true paranormal experience, but, not put off by my lack of ghostly expertise, NIPRA founder Warren Coates showed us around the castle on our arrival and joked he had removed all of the blood from the walls before our arrival. He has been visiting Ross Castle with groups from NIPRA for many years. He came across the castle by accident many years ago and has been coming back ever since.

"So much paranormal activity happened the first time I stayed here at the Castle," Warren said.

We were given the quietest room in the small castle, which was built on the foundations of the original chapel. I could feel the other half breathe a sigh of relief as we were told that no-one had experienced any serious paranormal activity in our room. Warren assured us that all we had to contend with were lights going on and off in the middle of the night, and doors banging open and shut of their own accord. Next door was the 'whisper room' where Warren was staying. Guests who spend a night there often awake to hear voices whispering and the cupboards loudly open and close in the middle of the night.

After a quick tour we ended up in the top room of the castle where we learned more about the estate's infamous ghost Miles "The Slasher" O'Reilly, who spent his last night on earth in this bedroom in 1644, before he died defending the bridge at Finea. O'Reilly's descendants then took over the Castle and had it restored.

The spirit of Sabina Nugent, the daughter of an English lord whose Irish lover drowned in tragic circumstances in a nearby lake, is also said to inhabit the castle. She is believed to have died of a broken heart and several members of NIPRA have heard a woman wailing on visits to the estate.

Warren and his colleagues began by conducting baseline tests in all the rooms to establish their temperatures before the night's main activities began. There were a range of devices used to constantly monitor the temperatures in each room to see if sudden drops in temperature coincided with any paranormal experience. Digital cameras are also set up in most rooms to record any paranormal activity.

At around 8.30 p.m. we all gathered in the main room of the Tower for a séance; a digital camera was set up to film the event in night vision as it was conducted in total darkness. Having never participated in one before I am not sure what I was expecting, but calling upon the spirit world in total darkness wasn't what I had in mind.

Not long into the proceedings one woman, also a newcomer, felt a hand brush against the back of her legs and, frightened by what had just happened, she soon left the room.

"I had actually sensed a spirit standing right behind her just before she had her experience," Warren told me. "Usually when we come to Ross Castle we get a lot of activity."

Taking a break in the Main Kitchen a little later on, Warren and Gary Waters, another long-term member of the group, said it was hard to always know what to expect at Ross Castle.

"We can never tell you what will happen beforehand," Warren said, "I would love to be able to tell you that this will happen at exactly this time, but it doesn't work like that."

Much later on in the evening we went into one of the main bedrooms, called the Cave Room. The name comes from the odd-shaped en suite bathroom, which has been built deep into a recess of the old castle wall. The room is less than two body-lengths wide and the room slopes down, so that when you are lying in the bath it feels like you are lying in a tomb. Our group sat in this room, again in the dark, and asked the castle's ghosts to make themselves known to us. The other half and I were sitting in the doorway into the Cave's bathroom; we heard quite a few eerie noises and sounds coming from the bathroom as the spirits were called forth to contact us. "We saw crosses right above that doorway," Gary said. The NIPRA monitoring equipment for the evening showed a dramatic drop in room temperature from eight degrees to minus two, around the time a member heard a woman crying.

We soon returned to our Chapel bedroom where we had a mostly quiet night's sleep. The next morning, however, the door to our room popped open by itself and we heard a thud-like noise that seemed to come from nowhere. A wee bit spooked, and tired from all the ghost hunting, we decided to hit the road and put an end to our encounter with the spirit world.

If you are into ghosts and scary experiences this is a great place to take a group of friends for what will surely be one of the weirdest nights you've had in ages; even just driving up to the old stone-walled entrance you feel as if you are entering another realm.

The castle itself is amazing and all the rooms are decorated with period antiques which the previous owners have collected over the years. There are lots of stuffed birds and small animals all over the place which adds to its old world ambiance. Walking the grounds is also very enjoyable, but be careful as the path is overgrown and slippery. For the full ghostly experience request a room in the main Tower, as these rooms not only have their own bathrooms, they are also the site of most of the castle's reported paranormal activity.

NIPRA runs weekend tours to Ross Castle and other homes and estates around the country; for more information about these events visit the Group's website www.nipra.co.uk. I am sure by what has been said in these last few stories that you won't be leaving disappointed!

These next couple of offerings are given to me by Kim Good of C.A.P.S. (Concorde Antioch Paranormal Society) which can be found in Northern California.

Where to begin? Let me start with the ghost girl in my house. We had just moved into our house and one night my husband was in the shower and I had gone to bed. It was 11.30p.m.

I was lying in bed and started hearing kids playing, and I am thinking to myself: 'but it's SO LATE, who is going to have their kids out at this hour?' Especially during the week, and it was not a holiday. I did have the TV on but it was on a music channel, so there were no kids' voices. So, I start to get mad as the noise was keeping me from sleep, so I get up and look out of the window and see nothing; no-one is out there and all the other houses have their lights off, so I go to the kitchen to see if I can hear anything in my neighbour's back yard, again nothing. I just decide to go back to bed. As soon as I lay back down I could hear the kids again, so I rolled over and saw a little girl standing in my hallway. She was wearing an old-fashioned white nightgown. She just turned and looked at me then walked away. I just turned over and went to sleep.

I have never seen her again, but I do feel her sometimes and she does like to hide things and then put them back. It drives us a little nuts, but it is nice to have her here.

Kim says: since we are Paranormal Investigators we have so many stories, and here is another good one.

This one is pretty recent and happened about a month ago. We were up in Ione CA, in the cemetery, it was about 10.00 p.m. We were just walking around and taking pictures and to see if any spirits would talk to us. I was reading a tombstone and a rock was tossed in my direction. No one I was with threw the rock. It happened about three more times and we started hearing what sounded like coins being flipped in our direction, almost like they were coming off the tombstones. It was a tradition, and still is in some places, to place coins on tombstones out of respect. For the life of us we couldn't find any of these coins we were hearing. One of our members may have it on video, but we are still going through the evidence.

So, we decided to go to the other side of the cemetery. One of our friends, a member of another Paranormal Group, had just said that she felt uneasy, so we turned to leave and a HUGE rock got thrown at us; it was like the size of half a brick, so we decided to go. At the gate to get out we heard a noise like a scream and then right behind me I heard a sound like someone had stepped on a branch, but there was no one there.

Back at the hotel, me and another member had a few more experiences. We were in the room and it was about midnight at this point and we were not tired after everything we had just experienced in the cemetery so we are sitting on the couch discussing the fun day we had ahead of us and we started to hear noises outside our door. We were staying at the Ione Hotel. There are only fourteen rooms and one room where the manager stays, and they are all upstairs. There are no elevators; only one staircase right up the middle of the hotel. I opened the door to see what was going on. First off all the lights were off on the floor where the rooms are. The keys are all old-fashioned metal keys, no fancy key cards, so we walk out.

All the rooms were closed except for one that was not rented out for the night. We could see all the rooms from where we were standing, some people were watching TV but quietly, there was no one out and walking around other than us. We went out on the back veranda and saw a shadow down below the balcony, then, the door started to shut behind us so we decided to go back in.

Once back in we were hearing footsteps from downstairs so we ran over to look. No one. Downstairs there is a restaurant which closes around 8.00 p.m. and there is a bar but the bar was closed as it was getting a new liquor licence. I was just staring down the stairs hearing someone walk around and seeing no one. It is the strangest feeling in the world to hear something your brain knows so much to be someone walking around and seeing nothing there. So, we decided to go back to bed as we had a long day ahead of us. All night we heard people walking up and down our hallway and the door handle jiggling. Oh, all this happened on Friday the 13th, the cemetery and everything at the hotel. The next night – everything was perfectly quiet and still.

The next stories are from Chris P. who lives in Texas with his wife. He has a passion for EVP's (electronic voice phenomenon), and has recorded many of them in his house. I think Chris might benefit from a full investigation and then shed some light on these happenings, if he hasn't had one done already! Chris says:

Odd things have gone on in our house: a few years ago my wife was out watering the plants in the front yard, when suddenly the water got turned off. There was no one around and I was in the house and I wouldn't dare do something like that anyway! I have a couple of EVP's where I'd asked who did it and got replies, which I can send if you want.

My wife and I were doing an EVP session one evening, sitting in our recliners, when suddenly we both smelled what seemed like hot chocolate. If I recall I captured an EVP during this time when we were talking about smelling chocolate, and that it was like a little laugh.

Every once in a while my wife would hear me calling her when it really wasn't me. For instance, I'd be back with my computer – which I usually am in the evening – and she would be in the living room watching TV. She would come back into the computer room and ask me what I wanted – and I had to tell her I didn't call her. This was happening once every couple of weeks for a while, until she got tired of it and told whoever it was to stop and it seems to have done the trick.

She was in bed one night (we sleep in separate rooms because I snore!) and she said sometime during the night she woke up to the sound of a little girl crying; she said it really frightened her.

We opened up the cabinet where we keep our pills one night and one of the pill bottles was stuck to the door. It just hung there. We finally pulled it off; we could find no reason for it and could not duplicate it either.

My wife has got her shirt tugged a couple of times when she has been outside, and I have one set of EVP's I like to call residuals, which if you listen to sound like noises inside the house where someone is washing dishes, pouring water and so forth.

So that is all I think of for now, apart from our Yorkie before he went blind. It seemed like he used to be able to see the spirits in the house. He would look up to the ceiling and seem to follow something with his eyes and at times be wagging his tongue. However, even now that he is blind, occasionally I'll notice him doing the same thing, so we are wondering even now that he is blind if they are still interacting with him somehow.

Chris also sent me this little "tidbit," as he calls it, and it says::

One night, maybe a couple of years or so ago, I came out into the kitchen to get a drink sometime after midnight. I hadn't turned on any lights yet but I could swear I could see the back door open with my wife standing there. I called out to her and got no answer. I did that several times. So, I turned on the light – the back door was closed and no one was there! Of course, when I asked her about it the next day she said it wasn't her and that I can believe, so I am not sure who or what it was.

Stephanie of P.A.C.T. Paranormal has been good enough to send me the next stories. She and her mother are co-founders of this group and they are based in Western North Carolina. She writes:

The first unexplained thing that ever happened to me was at the age of thirteen. I was lying down on my bed reading a book that I was assigned at school and my dog Juno was lying at the bottom of my bed chewing one of her toys. Juno suddenly jumped up and started growling and barking; she was looking at the floor. I crawled to the foot of my bed and looked where she was looking. There on the floor was a penny and it was "hopping" across the floor, the best way to describe it is that it would hop into the air and flip over and then land back on the floor. It did this a total of four times, which is when I yelled for my mother. As soon as I did that it stopped. I must admit I was freaked out, but that was all that ever came of that. I still think about it from time to time; it has been eleven years since this happened and I am still no closer to an explanation.

Stephanie tells me that the next story is what got her into investigations into the paranormal.

Back in March of 2009 it was late and I couldn't sleep. My ex-husband, his younger cousin and I decided we would go for a late night walk. It was a full moon that night and you could see everything as if it was daylight. We were walking on the main highway and we turned into a side road that looped back around to our home at the time. The loop was equal to about one and a half miles. As we began walking the guys started telling me about a house that used to be on this road and decided to show it to me, so we turned into this dirt road that went sort of uphill. As we reached the location where the house was, we noticed that it had burnt down and only the bottom foundations remained. We then turned back and went back down the road to where we were walking.

This was approximately midnight and, as we continued walking and rounded a curve, the guys were apparently feeling adventurous. There was a barn to our right and they told me they were going to check it out. For whatever reason I got a terrible feeling when this suggestion came up. In a bush next to me there was a bird that began going crazy. This struck me as odd but I insisted I didn't want to look at the barn without a flashlight. I proposed that if they would walk back and get a flashlight with me, I would return and check out the barn. They sort of laughed off my offer and decided to go on their own. I guess they were going to leave me standing there. As they turned to go toward the barn, one of them was looking down the road straight ahead of us. He said, "What is that standing in the road?" I thought this was an attempt to scare me. As I looked ahead I could see a very tall, slender shadow on the double yellow lines. I stood there trying to figure out what could be producing such a shadow and trying to figure out how I missed seeing it on the way down. That's when I was in store for a shocker. This "shadow" walked distinctly on two legs from its position on the double yellow lines to the white line on the road to its right; our left. It then turned to face us again. The guys had already took off running and I had a bit more of a delayed reaction. I then joined the guys not far behind. I looked back over my shoulder, as we were running, a total of three times. This "thing" was chasing us on all fours, but unlike any animal. The last time I looked over my shoulder it was just a couple of feet from us. It was featureless; just a very dark shadow. It then vanished before my eyes – it was not like it was something that ran into the woods or anything like that, this "thing" just vanished. I was utterly terrified, but this "thing" never left my mind, and that's when curiosity set in.

The following day I called my mother and told her what had happened. She then said we had to find out what it was. She demanded answers, and this led to another visit to this location.

The second visit drew a bit of a crowd; after telling our story to some friends they decided to join us on our next visit to the location. The group consisted of my ex-husband, my mother and three more friends. One of these was our elderly friend Midge, who has since passed away. The other two were our friends Margaret and her daughter.

We met at Midge's house and discussed our previous encounter. We all then loaded up and headed back to the shadow figure's territory. As we arrived, Margaret received a bad feeling and decided not to walk with us; she remained in her vehicle along with her daughter and watched from there. The remainder of us walked down the road and hoped for answers. At this point we weren't seeing anything. We were hearing a lot of noise but nothing that could be proved to be that of the figure. An overwhelming feeling overtook my mother and she was eager to get Midge back to the vehicle. We began walking back, which was uphill, and as we walked my mother and Midge stated they had seen two red lights in the woods that appeared to be eyes.

As we reached the vehicle, Margaret appeared distraught and she asked, "Which of you were wearing reflective tennis shoes?" The answer to that was: no one. She appeared confused and said she had kept up with us walking by the reflection off someone's tennis shoes. As she was telling us this, she pointed to another side road that veered to the right. She had watched this reflection going in the motion of someone walking down this road. In conclusion, not only did we not have anything reflective on any of our shoes, but we had not ever turned down that road that she thought she had watched us walk upon. That road goes to a camp ground which was behind a locked gate at the time. We still have no idea what she saw. On top of this, she then said she had seen lights bounce all around Martha's car. She also said she that she was never able to find a solution to what caused these lights to appear on mum's car.

As it reached time to leave, Midge was walking to mum's car to get in the passenger seat and we heard what sounded like huge crashing beside us in the woods, but could see nothing. The entire second visit was full of unexplained occurrences. Since these visits we have been back hundreds of times, and I shall tell you the most interesting occurrences among these visits.

During one walk through which included myself, mum and Margaret again, sticks began flying off the bank towards us. I was physically grabbed on the shoulder during one of our visits. We had walked to the house foundations I mentioned about earlier. We had a lot of guests on this visit and when we were walking back down, something forcibly grabbed my left shoulder. I thought it was one of our friends present, but as I looked back I noticed I was the last one going down; no one was behind me at all, or near me for that matter.

This location led me to form my paranormal team, P.A.C.T. Paranormal, along with my mum. Upon research, this location had quite a bit of history relating to it. The leader of the Kirkland Bushwhacker's (John Kirkland's) grandson was assassinated here as a result of an enemy seeking revenge. He was shot and killed in this very location.

This next offering is from Toby O., who saw my request for true ghost stories which I asked for from Twitter. He has been kind enough to send me the following:

I shall tell you my first experience of the paranormal; it is not a scary story, just spooky and I know that it was very real. I'll explain it in detail, so it will be very long.

My mum and dad separated in 1982 and later divorced. Me and my mum moved in with my grandmother and she lived deep in the country in a two-bedroomed ranch house. It had a den in the back which was made into a bedroom for me. Mum was one of eight children, seven of whom are still living. The one who had passed away was only two when he died, and this was before my mum was even born. On the wall, at the head of my bed, my grandmother had many family photos, one of which was Jimmy – the child who had passed away. That picture always spooked me. It was taken around 1939 in black and white but his eyes were a weird blue, like they were staring into your soul. I had friends in there that would not sleep in the room unless the photo was put away.

Anyway, my grandfather had passed away a couple of years before, in 1980. I was twelve at this time and had never had any type of paranormal experience before and wasn't scared of the dark or to be alone. At night I would lie on my back with my "boom box" on my chest and listen to music until I fell asleep. One night I had already put my radio on my headboard and went to sleep, when at some time in the night I heard what can only be described as pots and pans clanging together. Now, my bedroom had two doorways: one led into the hallway and the other into the kitchen. There was no light in the house; the only light was through the kitchen window and it was from a light pole two or three hundred yards away, so there was very little light but enough to make out the kitchen sink and counter. I heard that noise and opened my eyes, but the noise continued constantly. So I looked into the kitchen and there was a silhouette moving from the counter by the sink, then it would turn and bend over to the bottom drawer of the stove where the pots and pans were and then turn back to the sink again.

It didn't scare me; I just thought it was my grandmother – her nickname was Toots – and she had bad hearing. I couldn't figure out why she was up at this time and didn't have the light on, so I just said, "Toots," in a loud whisper. I got no response so I said it again in a louder voice; still nothing. I reached over and turned my lamp on and the noise stopped, and when I looked into the kitchen there was nothing; no pots, no pans – nobody. I got chills up my spine. I stayed there for a while, just thinking. I finally got the nerve to get out of bed and look closer but the kitchen was empty and clean. I eased into the hall and peeped into Toots' room and she was fast asleep. I even peeped into my mum's room and she was too. I went back to bed, and after a little bit I calmed down. I had school next day and needed to sleep, so I put my head on the pillow and turned my radio on low, reached over and turned my lamp off. The second it went dark the same noises returned. I looked into the kitchen real fast and that same image was there. Now I really was scared, and shaking. I noticed the image looked bald-headed. Anyway, whilst keeping my eyes on it I reached over with my right hand and turned the lamp on, and when my hand had gone back down, the silhouette just vanished before my eyes. Keep in mind I had never studied the paranormal and never thought about ghosts, and I can also tell when I'm dreaming and awake. I also dream in colour, which is rare from what I've read. Anyway, I'm not sure how long it took but I decided to leave my light on for the rest of the night and at some point I fell asleep.

When mum called for me to get up in the morning I jumped a little, opened my eyes and the very first thing I noticed was: my lamp was off. I thought to myself, did I dream that? No – I was wide awake; it was so real. I was at that age where I didn't want to wake my mum for such a reason and look like a scared little kid. I got up, picked out my school clothes and took them into the living room to sit in front of the heater to get dressed. Toots, who was around sixty-three at the time, was already awake and sitting in her recliner. She was always picky about making beds and cleaning up behind yourself, and not letting the dog sleep on the bed and leaving lights on. So, I sat there putting my socks on when out of nowhere she said, "Why did you leave your lamp on all night?" I think my heart skipped a beat, I don't remember what I said. I never told anybody until years later. I had kids of my own, even, before telling mum. When I did, she started asking all sorts of strange questions. She never admitted it but I believe she had seen and heard strange things there too. Toots, who is still alive today, is now ninety-six years old and has always been very religious – came right out and told me she knew the house was haunted and she still lives there.

I believe what I saw that night was my grandfather; he was short, bald and chubby – exactly what I saw. I think it was just a residual haunting, but who knows for sure? However, I have been woken up to a loud whisper in my ear so close I could feel breath on my neck, but that was another story.

This story was sent to me from Simon, who is a member of Y.P.I.R.A. which stands for Yorkshire Paranormal Investigation and Research Association. Simon tells me if you look up the Black Monk of Pontefract, you will find more details of the house there. He tells me:

Me, my partner, and another member of the team, went to 30 East Drive in Pontefract (you may want to look it up as it is now a B&B). We didn't get the chance to stop the night as my partner didn't feel well, but we did have the opportunity to look around and we were offered a drink. We were only there about two hours but while we were there we felt columns of freezing cold air, the lampshades kept moving and stopping of their own accord, and twice my friend felt something brush past him. All three of us heard knocking on the floorboards upstairs although no one was there. My partner had a constant feeling of sickness while she was there, as well.

These next offerings are from Gary Taylor, who I have had the pleasure of passing (quite) a few emails with. He is not a member of a paranormal group but does go investigating some cases with Steve and Sue of UK Shadow Seekers, who helped him out with a fundraising event he was involved in. Not all of this can be classed as paranormal activity, but I thought it was worth including for you to make your own minds up about what he told me.

I was born on the 31st December 1972. My grandad (my dad's father) died suddenly in 1974 or 1975 from electrocution at his home. My young brain had no understanding of what had happened; I was very confused as I knew something wrong had happened but I didn't know or understand what. At that age I probably wouldn't have been able to express myself verbally and I couldn't ask any questions. It was a very profound and emotional time, I just didn't understand why.

At some point I couldn't sleep so I went into my parent's room and got in bed with them. They both had their backs to me, sleeping on their sides. I couldn't sleep as I was wedged in between them; at that age I slept in the foetal position on my side, so I lay awake. The headboard of the bed was against the wall, facing the window. My mum still has the dressing table in the same place in front of the window. From out of the corner of the room my grandad was there; he walked past the bottom of the bed looking at me, he tipped his cap at me and then – wasn't there anymore! He didn't appear or disappear, he was just there and then wasn't. Right then I knew that everything was OK; this ended my confusion. I then fell asleep. I believe my grandad came to see me so he could calm my mind. On reflection I think this instance somehow opened up my mind to accept this type of incident as normal, it certainly was at the time.

From this point I can't recall any times or dates of any other incidents from my childhood, although I am certain that there were some, just can't grasp them from my memory banks!

I do remember very minor activity before puberty, again I thought it was normal so can't give more of a description than the following: my old bed had a headboard with fake leather cushioned padding which was red. From the inside of the padding I used to hear tapping. I would tap back, trying to communicate with whoever was doing it. This continued for a while, but I eventually became bored as I couldn't effectively understand what 'whoever' was trying to communicate to me. I ignored the tapping and eventually it stopped.

Incidentally, my dad worked nights at the mill. When my older brother was quite young he would wake my mother up screaming, so she would go into what is our middle bedroom and he would tell her about the old woman in the corner who was beckoning to him. My parents were the second owners of this semi-detached property, built in the thirties. It had been empty for over a year before they moved into it in the mid to late sixties; it took them almost a year of negotiating before a price was agreed on as it was in need of a lot of work. The prior owner was an old woman.

When I was eighteen I began working at the Belle Vue Granada Bowls in Gorton. I would finish college that summer. I was completing a National Diploma in Advertising and Design (I did spend two weeks working in an advertising agency and hated office work; from this I learned not to make a career out of a hobby – painting, sketching etc.). The bowling centre had been there since about the 1960's. Belle Vue was a famous attraction in this area, it was also common knowledge that the building was haunted – most staff experienced "Oggy's" presence. I asked if this was his real name but it wasn't; he was named this for a reason I can't remember. One incident was at closing time, when nobody was in the pits (which was the area behind the lanes where the lane repair mechanics stayed to repair any breakdowns). Only the emergency lights were on back there, and from lane 1 the staff who were left, including myself, could all see the shadow of a person walking behind the lanes. We could also hear the person's footsteps the full length of the lanes.

The staff room was in the cellars, where a generator and storerooms were. I entered the toilets and the neon lights would flicker on and off until they remained on. Each time they flickered off, the large shadow of a man was visible. My immediate thought was that it was my own shadow, however it wasn't, as I soon realised. At the reception booth (where all of the bowling shoes were on shelves), I felt the manager's hand rest on my right shoulder and he sighed in my right ear. My initial thought was, "What have I done now?" I turned around to tell him never to approach me like that again – but nobody was there! These are just minor incidents I witnessed; so many others occurred of a similar nature. I had an incident occur in the bar's cellar when I managed the bar. I particularly disliked going down there. The cellar was in two parts and some staff wouldn't venture down there; it had an awful atmosphere. Many minor incidents occurred down there – small objects moved from place to place, noises and similar occurrences. It was the only area that scared me – whenever I was down there I would constantly be humming or singing that song from the Jungle Book, the "Bare Necessities," just to distract me from being down there!

Finally, here are a few short experiences Gary has had in the past and what he says has made him more of a believer than he ever was before.

RAF HOLMPTON – HULL

This underground bunker was one of my first paranormal investigations; it was also the first time I met Lynne who has now been a friend for many years and is very down to earth. During the investigation a group of us were in a very large bunk room where the staff slept. I was lying on a bunk in the back of the room. Nobody was near me as the small group was gathered around Lynne, listening to her. I couldn't hear her – just a male voice talking to me. I couldn't hear his words and I was whispering to him to talk a little clearer as I couldn't quite hear him. Lynne then called out, asking who was in the back of the room? I introduced myself and she informed me that a man who had committed suicide due to depression from being in service was talking to me.

Lynne is deaf without her hearing aids, and even with them she is a bit "cloth-eared"! I believe that this man could relate to me as I have been taking medication for depression since I was young, which is quite ironic as I am not a depressive person by nature.

ROTHLEY RAIL STATION – LEICESTERSHIRE

Again, I was on an investigation with Lynne. Rothley Rail Station is probably best described as stepping back in time at this preserved station. During a séance I was holding Lynne's hand and another woman's. Both myself and the woman said in unison that we had just had the Blue Peter* ship shown to us. As this was happening my hands were moving behind my back to join Lynne's and the woman's. I wasn't consciously doing this, so Lynne suggested I enter the circle. I did this and knelt down.

I got the sense of a young boy and he was touching the hair on my head while running around me. The hairs on my neck and arms stood on end and I could feel this boy's excitement that someone was finally there to play with him. We later found out that Blue Peter had awarded a young boy one of their badges at Rothley, but we also found out that he had later died.

*BLUE PETER is a children's programme on TV in England which first started in 1958 and still shows to this day. They have competitions, roving reporters and a Blue Peter badge is awarded for notable achievements. They also have a Green Badge for environmental-themed achievements. They have introduced other colour badges over the years but they always feature the galleon logo. The show is named after the Blue Peter flag.

BOLLING HALL – BRADFORD

This Hall is beautiful and I have visited a few times. As with many investigations, either nothing happens, or small inconclusive events occur, or dramatic things can occur. At Bolling, all that happened was that a young woman was on a lone vigil but became afraid so left the room. Susanne – from UK Spirit Searchers – sent me in with no information.

Apparently I experienced what the woman had been scared of, I later found out. The presence of a man was moving around me with the intention of intimidation. I don't scare easily so I was quite "vocal" with him. I was having various colours of light shot at me but they were only small and did nothing but irritate me. Eventually the man gave up and disappeared down the central staircase.

STANLEY DOCKS – LIVERPOOL

This investigation is what began to change my beliefs,

although I may have got this one and Vane Tempest mixed up as I don't recall which investigation came first. Both were responsible for my change of opinions. Previously I had probably considered myself an agnostic, although I did know that ghosts and the afterlife were real.

At the Docks I witnessed what looked like a man doubled over and running the length of a deserted and abandoned warehouse. I then witnessed a face looking at me from within an open lift shaft. This (or Vane Tempest) scared me for the first time. I could see a darkness in the corner of the warehouse, so I decided to approach it. The best way I can describe it is that this darkness came rushing at me, gathering more darkness as it came. I shouted some profanity and ran away! I was then ribbed for being afraid for the first time and for the rest of the evening I was quite jumpy – to the amusement of my friend Denise and others!

VANE TEMPEST – DURHAM

This is an old barracks and we were in a circle conducting a séance and I was holding my friend Denise's hand and Lynne's. My eyes were closed and I could visualise that I had stepped back and I was within a tear between this world and the other. I was being pushed further backwards and I was fighting to stay where I was. Denise and Lynne were both aware of my struggle and were gripping my hands. I became quite afraid and opened my eyes. I still wonder what would have happened to me if I had just given up. It was a profound experience and I vowed never to return, but I did. Nothing happened on the next investigation there and on the first investigation we had some amazing Ouija board activity.

GORSE HALL – STALYBRIDGE

This investigation was in 2013 and I witnessed my first full apparition for some time. We were investigating the foundations of this old hall that was demolished a short while after the unsolved murder of George Storrs at the turn of the 20th century.

I had wandered off and on my return to the group I saw who I thought was Steve of UK Spirit Searchers, involved in one of his meditation sessions. I paid him no mind until I saw Steve about 80 yards away in a different direction! I then realised that the figure I had seen was wearing some form of black raincoat and black hat, both of which were wet.

I shouted to Sue (UKSS) what I had seen. I then learned that Steve had seen the same apparition a few nights earlier in the same spot – plus this figure had been observed by many others. The man was probably Storrs' stable man who committed suicide shortly after Storrs' murder. He was never a suspect and had a close friendship with his master, and it is thought that he killed himself as he blamed himself for not being there to protect him when he was most needed.

ATTINGHAM PARK – ATCHAM, SHROPSHIRE

This was at Christmas 2014. I visited here last year with my mum; we both have a passion for visiting National Trust properties and historic locations.

The Hall was busy and I was just leaving the servant's kitchen. A young girl ran across the corridor in front of me from one doorway into another. I thought nothing of it until I discovered the doorway which she had run out of didn't exist! My mum caught me up and asked, "What's the matter?" I replied that I had just seen the ghost from Christmas Past!

This next offering is from Mark Vernon, who is a private paranormal investigator who also deals with demons. I hope you enjoy this one as it is a little different! He is based in Wakefield, West Yorkshire, England. Mark has been kind enough to send me lots of pictures and although I can't include them here you can find them on his YouTube page.

It all started at the age of about eight years old. I would sit in a room full of people and hear voices and noises which nobody else seemed to hear. I learnt at that early age to stay quiet and not tell adults for fear of ridicule.

My first experience was in a derelict house's garden in Bradford. It had an ornate pond in which we used to catch tadpoles. We weren't supposed to be there. A noise caught my attention and on looking in the direction I thought it came from, no more than thirty feet away, I watched as a monk wearing a brown habit and walking a little Scotty dog on a rope lead walked past me. He appeared as solid as the dog. I was that close I could tell it was the same type of rope for the lead as he had around his waist. My first reaction was panic as I thought I had been caught. I could not see his feet or his face as he walked down the garden path past me and he took no notice of me. I watched him for about forty seconds, and watched he and the dog fade away into nothingness. I return often to the same spot in my adult years to see him again but, alas, it hasn't happened. The house was knocked down years ago and flats built there. I have asked residents who live there now if they have seen anything, but no luck.

I got invited to go and check out a supposed haunted

house in Wakefield, which I will call the "haunted cellar" or the "demon house". I have captured much evidence in there which is posted on YouTube. The lady who lived there was hearing strange noises coming from the cellar, things being thrown around and doors slamming, but whenever she went to check she found nothing was out of place and the noises stopped. She was beginning to get scared and hated being there on her own, so I said I would have a walk around and check it out. Within a couple of minutes of being there I got the feeling I was being watched but I didn't say anything. I don't like letting on to the fact to spirits/ghosts that I have the ability to hear them. I hear them when they talk and I hear them when they move around. I also see movement, but I won't go into that yet as I see things differently than most people. I asked the lady if I could have a cup of tea, but she hadn't any milk and said she would pop out to the shop for some. She said she would be about ten minutes, which left me alone in the house.

I made my way upstairs onto a landing and into a little bedroom which was empty. I shut the door and started doing an EVP/AVP session to see if I could tape any voices. I heard the living room door downstairs slam shut, then listened as I heard what sounded like a very large man climbing the staircase. At this point I thought to myself that the lady had not told me she had a boyfriend and was worried he didn't know about me and would mistake me for someone who had broken into the house. So I shouted out, "Hello, I'm the lady's friend," – no answer. The bedroom door was still shut. I listened as he got closer and the footsteps stopped right outside the door. Nothing happened for a few seconds and I shouted, "Hello," again, but still nothing. I opened the door to find nobody there. I first thought it was someone messing with me and had a quick look around but could not find anybody. At this point the front door opened and in walked the lady with the milk. I told her what had happened and she shrugged her shoulders and said that she hears that all the time. Now this place started to interest me.

I had my tea and while she watched TV she said, "Have a roam around and do what you want." I then went down to the cellar where most of the activity seemed to happen but I couldn't find the light switch as it was my first time down there, so I pulled my phone out and used its light to see by, while at the same time started recording for audio. I did this because I could hear people having a conversation about me. I was hoping to record it and on playing it back it was two men and a woman, or so I thought at the time. It turned out not to be the case! The two men were being nasty towards me but the woman intervened and told them to be quiet as she wanted to watch what I was doing. I heard her say, "I like him." One of the men replied, "Who, him?" which I thought was funny as I had no equipment or cameras. I asked the lady owner if I could investigate the house properly at a later date. We have become good friends now and I have been visiting the property for about three years.

I visited again with lights and cheap cameras and a camping chair. I often sit down there in the dark for many hours at a time, mostly day times as certain times are very active; this is because I believe this is the time the portals open up. Spirit energy and portal energy are very different. I can feel spirit energy and have proved many times on film when an orb goes past me; I point towards it for the camera, which shows I see them sometimes as well. As for portal energy – I cannot feel it but the portals do make a noise which I can hear. There are three in the house which I have discovered. The common places for portals are fireplaces and staircases. I don't know why that is the case, but I made contact with some genuine spirits there. At the time I asked the lady not to tell me any names of any relations who had passed over; I at first thought it could be her deceased family members trying to contact her. I was correct in that aspect – but there was so much more to come!

The spirits I contacted were genuine, as I have said before. I gave the lady three names which had been given to me and it turned out to be her mother, father and step-father. I did not know these names before. The lady was much more at ease knowing this, but I had not told her everything! I wondered about the other spirits who had spoken to me down there in the cellar that the lady had no knowledge of. Because I do what I do, and have visited many haunted locations, I knew it was strange. The house had three portals – normally it is only one.

I would describe the house as being like a bus station; many spirits passing through and sometimes I would speak to them only once and never hear from them again. But four names kept cropping up: Johnathan, Tyrone, Janet and Jacob. I found out from asking neighbours that the previous owner of the house was called Jacob Epperbaum. He had died of a heart attack on top of the landing by the little bedroom door way, the same place where I had heard the man's footsteps stop and the exact spot where he had passed away. It was many weeks before his body was discovered. Jacob was a very hard man to get talking to – sometimes grumpy and ignorant and I often heard him walk past me which I have recorded in front of independent witnesses in the cellar. He sometimes tags along on investigations with me. As for Johnathan, Tyrone and Janet: she seemed very pleasant but sometimes seemed to boss the other two around when they were nasty to me. She always would say she loved me and wanted me (which I thought was interesting!). I am always respectful to spirits and will speak to them as they speak to me, but these two guys were doing my head in! They threatened to kill me and made nasty comments aimed towards me no matter how nice I was to them, so sometimes I would lose it with them; I would pick a fight with them – it makes great recordings!

It was at this point I had started taking friends down

into the cellar. I just love taking sceptics down there. The shortest visit time down there was ten minutes and we filmed a shadow figure walking between us; the pictures ended up in the local newspaper. My friend Rachel was with me and taking pictures down there, when she caught something amazing. We didn't have a clue at first what we had caught on the camera. I sent it to Nick P asking if he had seen anything like it as he had worked in the Ministry of Defence in the UFO section and with him having strange pictures sent to him all the time – but he had not. I sent it to him as, to me, it did not look like a ghost or spirit and it had me a little bit confused. I did find out what it was in time – meet Janet!

After no luck with Nick P, I sent it to a guy called Don P, who ran a team called GSI Paranormal. He in turn asked if he could visit me with a team member called Tony R. Don was interested because, together with the photo I sent him, I also sent him some AVPs that I had recorded but could not understand what was being said on them. It was a different language; I knew it wasn't Latin as I knew a bit of Latin and would have been able to understand it if I heard it. Don told me it was Sumerian, the oldest language known to man. I won't go into much detail on this at present. While Don was there he filmed a shadow figure walking through the cellar as well. He also found two of three portals which were there so I knew he was quite genuine. He also told me about my three friends down there; he told me, "They may be pretending to be something that they're not," and I might be pretty upset about it when I found out.

It was later on in the week, armed with my new knowledge, I entered the cellar ready for battle. I accused them of trying to kid me and of the fact that I was on to them. It did not go as I had planned. Just before I was attacked I recorded an AVP between Johnathan and Tyrone saying, "Get him". Then it happened. I had never felt anything like this before and never again since that fateful day. I was standing in the cellar and what I can only describe as a "fog" – a very painful electrical energy – enveloped me and froze me to the spot. I could not control my body; I couldn't move. My head felt as if it was on fire. It lasted no more than five seconds but seemed like a lifetime. It is not that it scared me, but I felt really unwell and had to leave the house. It took about thirty minutes before I ventured back down there. The same thing happened again! So, I left again and did not return this time! This happened three days running but I was not going to give up and let them beat me. On the fourth day I told them I knew they were demons and I wasn't going away. I recorded Janet telling them not to touch me any more and the attacks stopped. Because of this I was feeling more confident and then started to talk to Janet.

One thing you have to remember about demons is they like to trick and lie and can do you some serious damage if they feel like it. Don't believe everything you read about them as most of it is nonsense, though sitting down there in the dark talking to her, I knew I had to do a deal with her which would benefit us both. I won't tell you what the deal was, but I can tell you I didn't sell my soul!

She told me it was her in the photo and her name was Kara, and I now use her as a bodyguard on different investigations including The Black Monk in Pontefract, one of England's famous poltergeist cases, which is another story. I have Brother Michael on film visiting the cellar, (he was accused of murdering seven young girls and biting their tongues out).

Back to the cellar – although Johnathan and Tyrone weren't allowed to touch me any more they started attacking visitors to the house, which I soon put a stop to through the way of Kara. I did say they were crafty. During my time at 30 East Drive I experimented in connecting a portal there to the cellar so that any entities there could come through and visit me. It worked, but then the two guys, Johnathan and Tyrone, got the East

Drive entities to attack, which I also stopped. Not good for business when all your visitors get scratched to bits. To this day I have not found out Johnathan and Tyrone's real demon names; they won't reveal them to me but they do have to do as I say, which I think is pretty cool! I know when they are around because these demons have a certain smell – and it is not sulphur, it is a little secret.

This next contribution is from Tony Parkes. He is a private paranormal investigator and he contacted me with this story after he had seen my request for stories on Twitter. So I thank him very much for this submission.

Most experiences of the paranormal seem to be in the dark, even more so when the weather would make Edgar Allan Poe smile. This one, however, was on a beautiful sunny day in Bristol on board the stunning, historic SS Great Britain.

My then partner, and now wife, and I were below deck taking photographs of where the armoury was displayed. A typical day out, until the lights seemed to dim and we heard footsteps coming down the stairs. The temperature cooled and the atmosphere seemed to me to become surreal, when three or four men came into sight wearing vintage Navy uniforms. One of them looked across at us as if we shouldn't be there. They attended to something behind a cabinet and left via the stairs they had come down. We carried on taking photographs but somehow something didn't feel the same. We commented to each other about their uniforms and that somehow, by luck, we had visited on a special weekend for the ship.

When we went up on deck things became a little stranger, as the staff were not in naval uniforms of any period! We wandered around, but still no uniforms. Later we realised that other than uniforms and the look of surprise/suspicion from one of the men, we couldn't describe them. We both thought there may have been four of them, but only three were really visible. Could it be that we both imagined the same thing at the same time? Could they have been ghosts? Or could, just for a few seconds, have time – slipped? I'll let you decide.

Hector has been kind enough to send in this next offering. He is from the Southern Arizona Ghost and Paranormal Society (SAGAPS).

I have many ghost stories from my adventures across the world but the ones here are closer to home and stand out the most. This one comes from Bisbee, Arizona, which is ninety miles from Tucson where my team is based out of.

During this time it was the monsoon season for us; thunder storms and heavy rain come pounding through the desert making it very eerie at night, which we love. Mostly because we believe that ghost activity is manifested through energy and, well, the static electricity that can emerge from thunderstorms is when we like to investigate.

The team this evening consisted of three guys and two gals. We pulled in to Bisbee; the town is small and originally a mining town, which is another thing we love. It was about 5.00pm, the sun is starting to go down and a small grey cloud passes over the top of us as we park our vehicles in front of the location we would be investigating which was the Silver King Hotel. We started unloading and unexpectedly a loud thunder crash bangs out. We all kinda jumped because it was so loud that it echoed in the small canyon we were sitting in.

We also believe that the geographical elements, such as rock and mineral, can conduct certain activity to occur in these parts. We all looked at each other for a moment and we all smiled. We had a good feeling about this investigation – I should have known something was setting us up!

We met the hotel owner and she showed us to our rooms. My co-partner and the younger female on our team all shared a three-bedded room as we had requested the most haunted room so we could run surveillance at night.

It turns out that a person in the late 1800's had committed suicide by running and throwing himself out of the window. As we listened to this story from the hotel owner I looked at the window itself and it was very wide and tall and the sill was very low, so running out of the window would be very easy to do and dropping from the third floor would mean a certain consequence: death. The man had apparently gone mad after his lover had betrayed him, so he met his fate in falling from the room we would be staying in. This bodes well for our team to get some paranormal activity caught on camera and audio. We unpacked, prepped our gear had some dinner and waited for the night to begin.

The problem with investigating the paranormal is you are surrounded by the elements around you; there happened to be a biker bar directly across the street which was loud and obnoxious. Us silly ghost hunters were NOT about to go over there and ask them to keep it down, so we waited until the bar closed at 2.00am. The noise contamination would be greatly reduced, thus giving us better controlled evidence if we caught any. This actually worked out for us since the dead of night, when all is silent, is what we anticipate. We want to hear the creaking of the building, the wind from outside hitting a shutter, hell – a mouse fart in the corner, even! It was now our time to begin the real investigation.

The building is very old and some of the floors were slanted which makes some of the rooms feel like a fun house (so to speak). This cannot deter from our focus though. We are a sceptical and meticulous group; we want answers and not just cheap thrills, so remaining still when we do EVP sessions is critical and also having our minds wander can interfere with the investigation.

The second floor is where the main office and some of the smaller rooms are. There was also a lot of restructuring going on in the rooms, two of which were being turned into a bar. We all know that changes in buildings, homes and locations can cause paranormal activity, so we focused our energy on those rooms first. No activity to be reported, though. The third floor was darker, not lit as well and had various rooms that wound into back rooms, but you couldn't tell this from looking in the hallway so we split up: three people on the third floor and two on the second. Yes, we tested out the sounds of the noise coming from our own footsteps and voices. We were all separated without "bleeding" into each other's recordings.

We got very, very creepy feelings sitting in any of the rooms at this Hotel – but still – no activity yet.

We took a 20 minute break to rehydrate and snack on some stuff. It was now 3.25am. Two people decided to call it a night and went to bed while myself, my partner and the youngest gal, kept investigating.

Earlier, when we arrived, the owner showed us a secluded area of the hotel which was cut off from the rest of the patrons to access, but us ghost hunters love those areas that have not been touched in a while and this part was definitely unscathed. There is a locked doorway which takes you into one of the original parts of the hotel, which had a bunch of old furniture piled up, with various items like broken mirrors, tables, chairs and couches. You could tell they were very old and no one had been in this area for a very long time. Dust was piled high in corners and on the furniture. Cobwebs scattered and blocked paths to walk into the room. We managed to get to a corner of the room and there lay a stairway. Decrepit, dilapidated and just friggin' scary! It led down so far and dark, our flashlights couldn't see the bottom. Apparently this used to be the stairway the miners used to use to get into the mining tunnel which was beneath the hotel. The workers would stay in the hotel and easily make their way back into the mines from there. Convenient for them, but now it was so rotted we didn't even dare go down it for the safety of my team, so we did an EVP session at the top and the mid stairs of the stairwell.

All is quiet; sounds from the noisy bar and bikers seem like days ago and a far place away from where we were at that moment. We began asking questions of the miners and their thoughts on the hotel which was being changed and how it affected their feelings. No activity in response to our questions, then our tech guy tried to provoke a response and asked, "Are you mad at the owners for changing the way this place used to look?" (Silent pause). "There is no need for miners anymore, so you can just get out of there!" (Silence for a moment). Just as he was about to finish with a third statement, "I said, GET OUT!" there was a big BANG! Just then something in the pile of furniture fell, dropped or moved and caused a loud ruckus to occur. We all jumped and of course, laughed about it. I commented "OK, the miners don't want YOU here buddy!" We finished our EVP session and left the area and went back to the hotel and our room.

As we sat in the room we noted how silent things were for the most part, up until we did a little provoking. It is usually not our style, but when you sit there and get bored in some places it is customary to try and stir things up, even if just a little bit.

Now, I have been in some very creepy hotels and locations and I usually have no issues getting to sleep, however, once we settled in and set up our audio recorders for the evening, I rested my head on the pillow and shut my eyes and these thoughts and words would come into my head as if something was trying to speak to me. Never before in my ten years of investigating had this happened to me. Random words which made no sense, like "charge", "rusted", "pushed". Just random thoughts that were so loud it was like a TV show was going off in my head if I closed my eyes. This had never happened before. Then the morning came. I had managed to get, like, three or four hours of sleep finally and we all met for breakfast and then headed for home back to Tucson.

A day later we began reviewing our evidence and the evidence we recovered from the stairway was shocking to me! Just prior to us beginning the provoking in dead silence, we were able to catch a couple of anomalies which still send chills up my spine. We caught a disoriented male voice, rough sounding but definitely clear syllables saying, "They are waiting," and a second piece of audio sounding like, "No sleep". Ack! Still, we had a very good investigation and a very cool payoff. I would guess the entity was very pissed off I had brought my tech guy into the area that might have been sacred to him.

The next crop of stories are from Jeremy Stark of the T.H.P.I., which stands for True Hunting Paranormal Investigations. He tells me the following:

I grew up in Houghton County, Michigan, in the USA. There is a little town called Lake Linden and in Linden is the second-oldest cemetery in the state.

It was August 2005 and I was out of school at the time and a buddy I had at that time, Joe, and I were kinda bored and just driving around in my car. I mentioned I enjoyed ghost stories and did a little ghost hunting every now and then, so he asked me if I wanted to go and check this place out. I think the name of it was The Holy Cross cemetery; I honestly don't remember as there are a couple of cemeteries right next to each other.

It was about 1.00 a.m. when we went in. The cemetery is built into a hill so I drove to the top, went around the loop and parked my car at the top of the cemetery facing the road. We got out of the car and just started walking around. This was my first time in a cemetery at night; just that kinda feeling alone is creepy. We started to read headstones to see if we recognised any names and took turns trying to scare each other. We were there for only about half an hour, then Joe noticed this large, oddly-shaped tree; he pointed it out and said, "Dude – that looks like the tree the headless horseman uses to drag people to Hell in Sleepy Hollow!" The creepy part of him saying that was he was right, it did kinda look like the tree from the story!

Since it was my first time in a cemetery at night and his too – we promised each other that, if one of us got too nervous we would leave – no questions asked. There would be no making fun of them for getting nervous or scared.

Well, after the tree comment my nerves were a little up because the whole time I kept thinking I was seeing things moving, hearing footsteps and hearing whispers. The classic ghost stuff that these days don't bother me one bit! So I said, "I'm done," and he agreed and we walked back to the car. Time for the creepy part!

The car is in sight and the moon is bright enough to see everything. All the windows of my car are fogged up. At first I just thought it was night-time mist on the windows. I go up to the driver's window and run my hand along, expecting to wipe the mist away. Nothing happened. I looked back at Joe, who was looking in disbelief. The windows were fogged up from the inside! All the windows were closed, so somebody had to have been in the car which wasn't possible as there were only two of us there! Then we both hear what sounds like a little boy laughing behind my car. Joe quickly looked and the laughing suddenly stops. There is no one there! He runs to the passenger side and we both get in. I shut my door and put the key in the ignition, and as I start my car I happened to look into the rearview mirror. In the back seat of my car is a little boy. He had a red-and-white striped shirt on, and black hair that came down to about where his eyes should be. I say should be because – he didn't have eyes and his face was paper white! He had no expression; he was just sitting there.

I screamed and hit the gas while the car was in park, I quickly jammed it into drive screaming the tyres and tore out of the cemetery. Joe was yelling and asking me why I was driving like that, then I told him what I had seen in the back seat. He told me there is an old story of a boy just like that, that a lot of people have seen at all times of the day and night. No seems to know who he is or was.

To this day, just thinking about this story gets my heart

rate going. The image of that kid sitting in my car fogging up the windows is gonna haunt me forever. To this day (ten years and hundreds of ghost hunts later) whenever I get in the car I brace myself and cautiously look in the back seat expecting to see him. I have even dared to go back there three more times: once with Joe again, and a college friend the following year, but we didn't see him; then with my crew T.H.P.I. four years ago – nothing. I want to go one more time with the crew I have now. They believe me and want to see him, but that is easier said than done now as I live some two hundred miles away from Lake Linden.

This next offering is from Jonathan Hastings, who is also a T.H.P.I. team member. He tells me this story:

We have many creepy stories and here is one that still scares Jeremy and I today. One night in Green Bay, Wisconsin, Jeremy called me and asked me if I wanted to investigate. So we packed all our equipment up; IR cameras, voice recorders etc. He came and got me and asked where we should go. I told him there is a place in Shirley WI and not far from Green Bay, maybe fifteen minutes. It has a cemetery with reported green lights and people getting an intense amount of fear, like they were being followed. So we drove over to this place and parked right in front of it and shut the car off.

All of a sudden we heard a loud and very long growl coming from what seemed to be the back seat. We looked at each other, saying, "F... this". We started the car and floored the pedal, and sped off doing 65 miles an hour for at least five minutes. So after that we turned the car off (we were still out in the country but at least five miles away) and we STILL heard it! It had followed us and it was just as loud as before, so we drove as fast as possible, hoping it would stop following us, back to Jeremy's. It finally stopped, and after that we said we would never go back there ever again. We drove past once more on a different day but nothing happened. We took it as a warning never to go back again and we haven't. We now call that Shirley Cemetery Hell Hound.

Jeremy has also been kind enough to send in this story. I hope you all like this one – it's got a doll in it! I consider them and clowns as bad as each other! You can keep 'em as far as I am concerned and this might explain why!

This one doesn't really involve my crew but rather my two daughters. Some neighbour's kids gave my oldest daughter, Dana, a doll last summer. It was rather raggedy looking, well-worn and Dana loved this doll. She named it Genevieve; she never really played with it though, she just kept it on display on her dresser. Well, six months later the same kids who gave her the doll demanded she give the doll back. They tried grabbing her and pushing her, trying to get it back. My daughter had just turned six and they were scaring her. While I am not the biggest guy, I am tall and proudly display the tattoos up my arms and do construction and have studied martial arts for more than half of my life. You had better believe that mess ended quickly!

It was then that I started to wonder what it was about this old doll that drove those kids nuts. Both my daughters began to fight over it (the girls are three years apart). The doll would always end up in the strangest places around my kid's bedroom. I was always scolding Dana for leaving her doll lying around, as I would trip over it constantly when it was dark. Dana would keep telling me she did not put the doll there, and it couldn't have been my other daughter Rachael because she wasn't tall enough to reach it. Then the nightmares began.

Dana would have very, very gruesome nightmares of Rachael being attacked by strange animals and then killing her, then her mother, then me, while they forced her to watch. She's six and I never expose her to anything graphic! I was starting to get worried about where these gruesome images were coming from. I tried to pass it off as she had perhaps overheard some older kids in the neighbourhood, but what Rachel did one day made it impossible to ignore.

We came home from dinner one night and Rachael was as happy as could be. Then she began to run into her room and stopped in the doorway. She let out such a scream and came running back to me. I asked her what was wrong and she looked up at me and said, "There's a man in my room". I quickly made everyone go across the hall to our friends until I came to get them.

I'm the kinda fella that always keeps a blade of some kind on me. I took out my pocket knife and went to my room where I keep my pistol. I take my pistol out and search the apartment three or four times. No sign of anyone and no sign of any break-in, but in my daughters' room it felt about twenty degrees colder than the rest of the apartment. I go across the hall to get everyone, then I get Rachael to describe the man. She told me he was tall like me, with green skin and long white hair.

Days go by and Dana's nightmares get worse and Rachael keeps saying the green man is in the closet. My evenings were spent sitting in their room until they fell asleep. One day, after dinner, the girls were playing in their room when both of them screamed and ran out to me saying the man was back! Rachael looked at me and asked me if I could take my sword and get rid of him. So I figured I would make a little noise in their room and that would make it stop. I take my sword, as well as an empty CO_2 pistol, and go into their room and shut the door. I kicked some things around to make some noise and a little show for them to have some peace of mind. I called out, "Alright you son of a bitch, show yourself!" and fired my CO_2 pistol a few times.

The Genevieve doll was on Dana's dresser next to the closet. The room instantly became cold enough that I could see my breath and my skin began to hurt. My eyes locked on that corner and I watched as the doll's whole body turned almost ninety degrees to face me. There was a loud POP and the lights went out. At that moment it all made sense why kids obsessed over this doll, why my girls were having nightmares and seeing things.

I quickly left the room and went into the kitchen, grabbed a paper grocery bag, a container of sea salt and a stapler. I went back into the room and the lights were all on again. I carefully reached for the doll, but as soon as I touched it I began to feel sick; I was light-headed, sweating while being freezing cold and felt like I could vomit at any moment. I picked the doll up and poured some sea salt into the paper bag to line the bottom. I tried to put the doll in but suddenly one of the doll's arms would jerk up and catch the top of the bag. I tried it at a different angle – its leg would suddenly stick out. This doll was actively trying NOT to be put in the bag! Finally I set the salt container down and with both hands I shoved the doll in. Right away I pinched it shut and emptied the stapler into it.

I called up one of the guys from my crew and asked if I could store the doll there until I figured out what to do. He was fine with it. I put the bag in the trunk of my car. My car, which was in top condition, didn't want to start too easy. Steering was hard and the breaking was uneven – I was glad he only lived five blocks away! I told him what had happened and he agreed to hold the doll until after the winter was done.

Once the winter was over we went out into the middle of nowhere with a cooler, superglue, rope, a letter sharing this story, salt and a shovel. It was that night that my friend and T.H.P.I. crew member, Mike, noticed weird things happening with the doll. We quickly put the salt in the small cooler along with the doll and the letter. I superglued the lid shut and then proceeded to tie the cooler. I dug a hole deep enough to take the cooler and we jammed it in and covered it. Then we found a heavy rock (around 250lbs) and rolled it on top of it. I said a blessing over the area and we left.

I never told my daughter what happened to her doll, but she only asked about it once though. The nightmares stopped and the green man with the white hair hasn't come back.

So, that is the story of the doll. I always thought it would be cool to see a doll move by itself but it is not – it's REALLY creepy!

GHOSTS, DEMONS AND DOLLS

Mike Bagozzi who is also from the T.H.P.I. crew has sent in these stories. They do seem to be a very productive team and he also says that the team has been on TV on the 'Monsters and Mysteries' series with stories about a Hell Hound and the Ghost of Mary Dean. Mike now gives you these offerings. Mike says:

It was one night late last year; it was about eleven or twelve at night and I felt something in the apartment. I never feel things, even on hunts; Jeremy and Jon go on and on about how the air is strong and heavy and I never notice a thing! But tonight I was feeling so incredibly anxious that it got to the point where I took a weapon and searched my apartment room by room checking for intruders. I found nothing. So I went to bed but I was still feeling anxious so I set up an EVP app we use on hunts, to see if I could catch any words. Usually we get about one word every five to ten minutes, within half an hour I got over forty words, seven which made sense. I got the words "Greece" (I have dozens of books on Greek mythology), "Hangers" (my bedroom floor was covered with hangers), "Lunch" (I had recently written a note to myself so I wouldn't forget to bring lunch to work the next day), etc.

I couldn't sleep, so I got up to get a drink. As soon as I walked into my living room (all of my lights in the apartment were off) I noticed it was brighter than usual. My desktop screen had turned on. The only way for it to turn on is to click the mouse or hit a key. I hadn't used it for hours so there was no reason for it to be on. I was getting pretty freaked so I turned my hallway light on; not much light but enough to relax me a little. I got my drink and headed back to my room.

My back was to my computer (still lit up) as I turned the hall light off and saw the shadow of a person out of the corner of my eye, right in front of my computer! I turned towards it but there was nothing there. I immediately went into my room and shut the door, and somehow I managed to fall asleep. The EVP stayed on all night but didn't get any more relevant words. The next morning all anxious feelings were gone and all was normal. I have never felt anything that strong since then.

GHOSTS, DEMONS AND DOLLS

This is Mike's second story and he says this is just as scary as the Hell Hound incident.

My friend A, who found out I was a paranormal investigator, told me that her little sister, who was 15 years old, was possessed and had been for some time. I was of course sceptical at first, but the events of that night proved her right.

Another friend, D, was also interested in the paranormal and for a birthday present I agreed to let her come with me on this night. We got to A's house after dark and I could tell immediately that her sister was strange. She constantly eyed me as if figuring the best way to attack. It sounds paranoid and exaggerated, but that is the vibe I got.

We wandered through the house, including the basement. There were shadows and such in the basement but nothing too serious, until her sister decided to allow a spirit to speak to us through her! I was so put off by her behaviour that, as a precaution, I hid a knife in my sleeve. Obviously I wasn't going to stab a 15-year-old girl, but it made me feel safer.

Her sister sat on the edge of the basement fireplace and answered some questions through the spirit, her eyes locked with mine the whole time. As I said in my previous story I don't get feelings or see/hear much on hunts, so you can imagine how I felt when my head filled with a vision. I could tell it was the sister giving me the vision. I saw her get up, grab a free weight off the ground and bash D in the head. The entire time she was communicating with the spirit, the girl's finger was drawing a shape on the fireplace by her leg. We never figured out what the shape was; she didn't even know she was doing it.

After the session, the girl said to me, "Don't be so obvious". She was referring to showing how protective I am towards D, including the knife in my sleeve.

We decided to get some McDonalds for dinner. D and I drove separately to A and her sister. I decided to call my friend, M, who was living at my house at the time, and tell him to check on my mum to make sure she was O.K. My phone was plugged into my truck's sound system. I called once but his phone rang out. I called again and it rang twice – followed by a loud screeching noise and random beeps. That has never happened before and never has again. I finally got hold of him after that and warned him. We talked for a while but decided to call it quits after that.

I was driving D home when I got a phone call from A. Her sister had gone into a fit, drawing with a Sharpie on the kitchen table and whimpering pathetically. I don't remember the exact words she said but it was something like, "God took my baby!"

The next day, D told me her mother had been freaking out as D hadn't been answering her calls. Her mother had a nightmare that D got her head bashed in that night. I checked out the case a few more times, but nothing much happened after that.

This is my only solo investigation and one of the only investigations I have been legitimately scared on!

Paranormal teams seem to be a very good source to get a creepy story or two from and these next stories are no exception. They are from a team called CULZ Paranormal, who are based in Castle Rock, Colorado. This offering is from Alan H and he says:

During one of our investigations we had one of our most remarkable experiences to date. It is one thing to hear EVP's and to see shadows on the cameras, but to have it happen and experience it live takes it to a whole new level.

The first happened in the old barn just behind the main location. My brother, Adam H, and Scott K and I were wrapping up an EVP session and thinking about heading back when we realised something was holding the barn door shut. We took turns trying to get it open but we couldn't get it to open, just like someone was hanging on to the other side! We tried de-bunking it seeing if it could have grabbed on something or simply been stuck, but every time after we finally got out, it opened and closed without any problem.

What followed in the basement in the main location was beyond words. We were running a full spectrum camera session, trying to make contact with the spirit of the woman who had been the former home-owner there. We started to hear these footsteps and used the walkie-talkies to determine that the other two parts of the group were nowhere close. So we asked who was there, and the footsteps were getting louder to the point where the sound came from just feet in front of us. It sounded like wet rain boots slapping against the concrete floors of the basement. During the research we found out that the basement had at one point been partially outside – which could explain the sound of rain boots.

This is another from CULZ Paranormal and this one is from Keegan C. What he tells us is:

One experience that really sticks with me is something that happened back in 2011.

We were investigating a location that had all the build-up of a true haunting. The story goes that a man took kids up to the first floor of a house and they all burned to death in a fire. Whilst, after doing some research, the story seems more urban legend than hard fact, it doesn't take away the fact that the former land owner did have kids who died on the property of unnatural causes.

We were making our way up the trail; Sam was in the front with the spirit box, I was in the middle with the EVP and Josh was last with camera duties.

The forest was calm as it was a clear night with no wind, and stars dotted the sky like raindrops on a windshield. We had just made our way out of the long brush and thick scrub oak into a clearing where we could see all of Castle Rock. The moon was lighting up the scenery and it was a perfect photo-op and video session to see if we could try and get some EVPs. Not having any luck, we decided to push on and follow the trail going into the woods. As we zig-zagged our way through the brush we asked the normal set of questions: "Is anyone there?"; "What is your name?" Still having no response we continued our trek, always keeping a good idea of our surroundings as the path was littered with rocks.

Suddenly, all the hairs on our necks got raised, and an eerie feeling of being watched grabbed a hold of us. We stopped to look around, and we asked some questions and moved the flashlight around. Being in the woods, which were home to bears, pumas and coyotes, we always had to be aware and careful. The feeling went away and so we carried on, but with every step we took something mimicked us and made the same movements, maybe five to six feet off trail! We kept stopping and looking, but never could we see anything. We radioed the other members of the group to see where they were and they were all back at the location that we deemed the Basecamp some two miles away. It clearly wasn't them so, honestly, at that point we started to think it could be an animal. We kept lights on the brush to see if we could see a reflection of eyes.

We started nearing the part of the path that makes a sharp dip to the left and heads west next to the creek and the sounds were only getting louder and closer! Whatever it was, it was clearly getting more and more interested in us. The EVP was running the whole time so we stopped and I pushed 'play' to see if maybe it was spirit activity after all, and then the walking sound in the forest became a dead-full-on sprint towards us! Josh and I jumped around to face it and Sam soon followed suit. At that moment I thought a cougar or bear was about to leap out at us, but as soon as the noise burst out into the open we didn't see anything but the slight movement of grass and branches and heard the sound of something running through the creek on the other side!

We stood there, all shocked it wasn't an animal but a spirit that had been watching us the whole time and that had charged at us! We looked in the dirt and mud for footprints but didn't find any.

It was a moment of investigating I will never forget in a location that always seems to have a trick up its sleeve. Not only have we encountered that, but we have captured our best EVP to date and at the same time on camera we caught a spirit passing. As well as an investigation we did where some teens had used a Ouija Board and been followed home by spirits, when we came into contact with something odd (the Ouija Board obviously had something strange with it as, whichever car we put it in, the car had immediate failure equalling being totalled).

This next story is from Colin C who is also a team member of CULZ Paranormal. It is not a long story, but not something I would want to happen to me! He tells me:

This will be one of the most memorable ghost encounters I have ever had. I wasn't sure of the exact time but while I was in my bed sleeping, I awoke to a noise. Nothing happened and after about two minutes I started falling back to sleep, and then the front corner of my bed started to sink down. It sunk down so much I actually started falling into it! I didn't have the guts to look and eventually I went to sleep. To this day I am not sure what it was – but I'm not sure if I wanted to know anyway!

Keegan has also added a little bit to this story and says that whatever it is in Colin's house, it has also been known to throw things off shelves and it also has a particular attraction to a model helicopter which it seems to enjoy throwing around too!

Here is another offering here from Mark C, again with CULZ Paranormal. This is what he tells me:

A haunting experience that stands out with me is when our team went out to a location near Parker in Colorado. The location had many gruesome deaths, which can breed hauntings. One was someone who was strangled while being pulled behind a truck; another was a body that was found in a bag with a rope tied around his legs. Another person was murdered there which turned out to be someone related to a co-worker, and just a mile away was a car crash which killed some teenage girls in the 90's.

We started the investigation near where the girls had crashed on the anniversary of the accident. It was a very cool and clear summer night as a large thunder storm had passed by just a few hours before. The gravel and dirt was clearly seen by the light of the full moon. While we got some voices and movements of leaves and, may I add, some crazy cloud formations overhead, we all decided to move on after Keegan C kept feeling like a spirit was calling to him. That's when we caught some EVP's at the second location.

During a follow-up investigation we kept hearing a truck coming towards us, but no truck could be seen. Out there you can see for miles as it's in the country and any car lights are also automatically seen. Then, after about 20 minutes we saw a flat-bed tow truck. There was a strange glow to it coming from the cab; all the lights on the outside were off. It stopped directly in front of us, and then drove by us with no driver! Can you say it was a ghost truck? We were all silent until Nick spoke up, "That didn't seem real!" To this day it is one of the craziest things I have ever experienced during an investigation!

This again is from a CULZ Paranormal Team member, this one is from Scott K. This an experience he had and says:

When the newspaper printed the picture and story of the bent and burnt bars of the front gate of Resurrection Cemetery, with the assumption it was made by the resident spirit called "Resurrection Mary," it caught my attention. I went there to check it out for myself to see what the truth of it was. The bars looked like a pair of hands had pulled and spread them apart. This started happening as soon as the cemetery had started to close and lock the gates; they never had been before, even with the spirit of "Resurrection Mary" hanging around.

It is my belief and many in the community that it was Mary herself who had pulled the bars apart. Workers came in and took the bars and straightened them, but they continued to change to a rust colour in the same spot no matter what measure were taken to put them right again. This continued to happen until they were eventually replaced altogether.

Again CULZ Paranormal has given me another story, this time it is from Aaron B, who says:

The night we investigated the Bonny Brae Tavern in Denver Colorado for the second time, our team was short-handed, as only three of us could make the trip. Being short of team members I think helped, because of the structure's size.

A little bit of history of the Bonny Brae Tavern: it has been owned by the same family and passed down through generations. It has been in business for more than 80 years, owned by originals Carl Dire and Sue Dire and later passed down to Hank and Mike. The establishment has had many regulars with many stories and became a Denver landmark.

When we arrived we set up our equipment and went our separate ways. Alan had a camera and an EVP recorder, Cory had a recorder and I had a camera and recorder. The night seemed pretty slow and there was not a lot of activity present and we all kept it pretty routine, asking for the presence of Carl, Sue or Hank. Also, we asked if any regulars would like to share a story or two.

At one point I walked over towards the men's rest room as I could hear the door shaking slightly. Previously, I had heard a former employee's claim of having been shoved into the door by an unexplained force, I began an EVP session. I didn't hear anything with my own ears and finished the session. I called Alan and Cory down the stairs and told them about the door. Alan got out his flashlight and set it on the end of the bar facing the men's rest room. Alan then requested the presence of any spirit to use the flashlight to answer any questions. In about less than a minute the light flickered on, untouched! We all got very excited and asked more questions and the light remained on. We ended the night with a spirit box session in Sue's favourite booth, but no evidence was captured through the box.

Later, over the next couple of days, the team reviewed the footage and they found some of the best evidence I have ever seen or heard since joining! Over by the men's rest room I had asked, "Is that you who tapped in the men's room? Can you do it again?" A class A EVP responded, "I was there" – that brought shivers down my spine! The second piece of evidence was the flashlight (next to the men's room). Finally, during the spirit box session, we captured on video a shadow running from right to left towards the men's bathroom. It was hard to see and we checked out any way of debunking it, but a person would have to physically run right in front of the camera to cause that, showing themselves along with their shadow. Great night – great evidence!

At this point I feel it should be said that I think the whole team of CULZ has managed to contribute a story for this Anthology. I would just like to thank them very much and say that they have been most prolific in their submissions and it is very much appreciated. Thanks again guys – and happy hunting!

The next stories are from a lady called Brenda Newby. She belongs to a team called SPIRIT Research Team, which she is involved in with other members of her family. These stories are supplied by her mum, Mary Jo, who is their Case Manager. They are from their Blog site (which is continually being hacked so they have taken the site down for a while) and she has kindly said that I can include them for you here. This team are from Dallas in Texas.

The position of Case Manager is certainly important in any investigation team, however it is not nearly as exciting as being on the actual investigation. As Case Manager I take all the photos and research the investigation sites, document positions, and record team activity. For this investigation I was using a point and shoot camera, with no frills, on a tripod.

The client in this case reported frightening shadow figures seen to peer into the windows at the back of her home at night. The figure was very, very tall and slender with a flat head and no apparent features. It was so tall it appeared to stoop over to look into the dining room window, frightening both the home owner and the "guard cat".

First thing next day, the home owner installed shades on all the previously uncovered windows, which faced an acreage with no nearby homes. However, she continued to feel a dark presence and on one occasion spotted the tall shadow figure moving quickly across the back yard as she exited a utility building behind her home. It ducked behind the garage to avoid being seen, most frightening!

The team's first task was having the team medium, Amy, walk through the home and through the back yard to get a feel for perceived activity and hotspots. I then took my camera and mounted it on a tripod and began photographing a series of shots, moving around the area methodically. Sometimes while doing this I will decide arbitrarily (ya think?) to take a few extra exposures of an area, or perhaps a different view of a specific spot. It was still daylight as I stood near the back of the barn and I simply turned around and took three magic shots, at a narrow area between the back of the barn and the tool shed. Only small pots and gardening paraphernalia were stored there on the ground – we all have that spot, don't we? Nothing came out of the blue and hit me in the head or pinched the back of my neck; nothing was whispered in my ear or pulled my hair – it was just an impulse.

Upon reviewing the photographs later, a shadow appeared moving against the wall of the tool shed. Aerial and ground photos proved there was nothing around the spot to cast a shadow on this wall, or even light hitting the wall to warrant the shadow. Granted the shadow is not 8-10 feet tall as the home owner reported, but it WAS moving.

The entire investigation proved to be a difficult and distressing case: investigators witnessed shadows moving about in a large tree that was central to the investigation and we believe voices in the captured EVP were not who they claimed to be. Stress and agitation marked the whole investigation; this shadow creature was up to no good and we left it alone.

SPIRIT's lead investigator, Brenda, advised a cleansing of the property and contacted a local parish priest to bless the home. Some spooks are better left alone!

This next story is also from Mary Jo from SPIRITS. In this one she tells us:

My daughter, grandson, his friend and I splurged on two rooms in the historic and reportedly haunted hotel in Jefferson, Texas. Jefferson is famous for its colourful history, lovely homes and Bed & Breakfasts, and – yes – its ghosts!

This small East Texas town has hundreds of documented ghostly apparitions and paranormal events; one of the hottest events is the Historic Jefferson Ghost Walk and another is the Excelsior House. The rates will scare you silly even before you get to your room! My daughter and I shared a downstairs room, the Victorian room, which featured a door opening on to the hotel's central courtyard, a king size bed, and the kind of tiny bathroom which is found in buildings which had no such convenience originally, with an elevated floor to hide the pipes.

We had taken the Historic Jefferson Ghost Walk, and we were exhausted and creeped out at the stories she had been sharing on dark street corners. My daughter hit the bed and promptly passed out; me – I was exhausted but doomed to roll around and relive the busy day. The room is almost dark and the bathroom light is on, the window unit is noisy. Being the age I am, I am thinking of making a bathroom run and turning the window unit to a lower temperature. That is when someone sat down on the foot of my bed near my foot! It – whatever – did not just sit down but did a little bounce, to boot! It took a few seconds for the terror to set in. I opened one eye – yes indeed, my daughter was on the other side of the bed, stone asleep, not moving. I didn't either. I froze and squeezed my eyes shut and suddenly I did NOT need the bathroom and certainly didn't think it worth getting up to change the temperature! I considered putting a hand out to shake my daughter awake, but no part of me would move. I never looked at the foot of the bed to see what friendly apparition had followed us back or, worse yet, lived in the room. I finally went to sleep in that position but boy – when I woke the next morning I was really hot and I REALLY needed to pee!

The next trip we shall stay across the street at the Jefferson Hotel – ha ha! It's haunted too!

Mary Jo has been kind enough to also give this story, which she hopes you will enjoy. She says:

I have always been intrigued by the possibility of ghosts; real ghosts. As a child in a small town in the 50's I would sit through horror movies and squeal with delight at being frightened by vampires, werewolves and the occasional alien. Walking the two blocks home alone in the dark (we could do that then), I would walk out into the street away from a row of hedges or a parked car, just in case one had followed me from the theatre and was waiting to jump out for real! Alfred Hitchcock would have approved of that, I imagined.

During my first visit to Jefferson, Texas, I ventured out into the dark – not alone this time, but actually seeking that elusive spirit which would jump out and scare me for real. We had taken the town's most popular Ghost Walk and my compadres were disappointed that the Ghost Walk did not include the famously haunted Grove House that evening so we set out to do a drive-by.

It was after midnight and the house was dark but there were plenty of lights around the exterior, including a street light. At the side of this charming 1861 clapboard home is the remnant of the garden: trimmed shrubs, bushes and trees, a couple of distinctive bird baths and a patio table. A spotlight shines down into the garden from the eaves of the house. It is in a small dark side street and very quiet. We stopped the car in the middle of the street, drove by slowly, backed up and repeated quietly. With the windows down we snapped pictures with our cameras using a flash (click, click, click).

Fast forward three days: I downloaded the digital photos onto the laptop and began flicking through them. Lots of dark Ghost Walk photos and some fun ones of the group and the occasional, "What was I thinking?" snapshot! I sped right through the Grove garden photos and then stopped – what was that? Back three photos and there he was! The man in the garden at the Grove – just standing there, appearing to hold a lantern, balding, long top coat, almost full body. OH MY GOODNESS! I called my daughter and she said, "Oh my goodness," (well, sort of!). There are no words to words to describe the feeling of having caught that image on my little point and shoot camera, with no flash.

We sent the photograph to the owner of the Grove, Mr M.H., who is also an author. His comment was, "One of the most compelling photos of our man in the garden." Nothing out of the ordinary for him; visitors and guests often capture this gentleman in their photographs, sometimes in group shots – but quite out of the ordinary for this group of spirit seekers. Look out, Bigfoot!

While I was trawling Twitter one day, looking for people to contact about true encounters and experiences, I came across Brian Holloway who is an Englishman from County Durham in the UK. He moved to Gibraltar, which is very near my home in Spain. He is in a TV show in Gibraltar which is called 'The Ghost Trail,' on which he is a co-presenter. When he is not investigating with them, he is in a paranormal group called Soul Seekers, along with his wife Giselle. He is a very busy person but was good enough to take some time to let me have a chat to him. I have put this together and it is the story he told me of what happened to a couple he knew in the UK. They found he was a paranormal investigator and as they got to know him, they started to mention the things that were going on at their house. This is the story of what happened when he went to investigate.

The couple of people we had made friends with were called Andrew and Stacey. They knew we were very interested in the paranormal and said that it was something they were getting interested in too. Brian described what went on at an investigation and Andrew and Stacey started to open up about the strange things that were going on at their house. Brian didn't think much of it at the time, but said he would go and see what it was that they thought they had going on, and try to debunk what he could and put their minds at rest.

Brian and Giselle went over to the house and Andrew and Stacey started to tell them about a problem they were having with a cupboard in their bedroom. The door wouldn't stay closed. Every night they closed it and every morning it would be open.

Brian said, "OK, is there anything else happening?" Andrew and Stacey then told them about the weird balls of light they kept seeing floating around all over the house.

At that point Brian thought it would be worth taking a more in-depth look at what was going on there. Andrew seemed to be more of a sceptic than Stacey. The occurrences seemed to affect her more than him anyway. Andrew did tell Brian that he was hoovering in the hall one day when he saw Stacey walk past the end of the hallway; he only saw her from her shoulders down as he was concentrating and looking at the floor. He called out to her but she didn't answer. So, he turned the hoover off and called again. That was when Stacey answered – from behind him and upstairs! Andrew said it was then that he started to think something was not right. He tried to rationalize what had just happened, as that was the kind of person he was, but he couldn't. He said to Brian, "I know what I saw. She was even wearing exactly the same clothes, but it couldn't have been her."

Brian told Andrew that he thought there was definitely something going on that was "not quite right," and that they would go in and conduct a full investigation. They arranged all the details then left.

At the time arranged Brian and his wife went to the house. Brian went in and sat on the couch and started to tell Andrew and Stacey how he had planned the investigation to go. No sooner than he had sat down than he felt extremely uncomfortable; he felt as if someone had just put their head over his shoulder and was breathing near his ear. Brian said that he never gets those types of feelings and, in doing what he does for a living, he doesn't scare easily. He didn't know whether to jump up off the couch, but realized if he did so Stacey would scream as she was aware something was very wrong; when he looked at her she was looking back at him with eyes the size of dinner plates! Brian said that he knew there could be nothing there in reality as the couch was positioned with its back flush to a wall.

Brian realized the situation had to be sorted out. But

this was the initial thing that made him think that he had really got something wrong that needed to be rectified. He had no idea at that point as to how bad things were going to get. And it did get really bad.

Brian decided that it might be better to leave bringing all the equipment into the house but just to do the investigation with Giselle, Andrew, Stacey and himself. At that point they arranged another night to go back when all the street noise had abated so there would be no interruptions.

The very next day Brian says that he got an extremely panicked phone call from Stacey. It was the middle of the day, she was a complete mess and in tears. Andrew was at work and she didn't know who else to call. Brian went over to the house straight away. He was wondering what had happened as he was only there the night before. He asked Stacey what the matter was. She said that she had gone up to the bathroom for a shower and closed the door. She was the only person in the house. It was then that she heard footsteps coming up the stairs – and they stopped right outside the bathroom door. The bathroom door handle began to shake and rattle like someone was about to come in. Luckily the door didn't come open, but Stacey was scared stiff. Brian then did a complete sweep of the house but found nothing wrong and no one else in the house. Brian thought it may have been her imagination running away with her. He told me that he doesn't always believe what people tell him until he has hard evidence, but she was in an awful panicked state. He told her that he had looked thoroughly all over the house and had found nothing wrong or out of place. After calming her down, he left.

A short while later Stacey called again and she was in as bad a state as she had been previously. She said this time she had been locked in the bedroom. She had gone in and closed the door, but when she went to leave – the door wouldn't open. She pushed and pulled at it and shouted for help. The door suddenly came open!

It was clear to Brian from that time that whatever it was, was focusing it's attentions on Stacey. Other things also happened before the investigation proper got underway.

Brian said to me that things in the house built up gradually, for instance Stacey was in the living room and could hear noises and her bakeware and kitchen utensils moving around in the kitchen. She went in to see what was going on – only to find nothing had been moved and no one was in the kitchen. Everything was exactly where it should be and where she had left them. The noises had also stopped. She went back into the living room. Again the noises and movement of the cookware started again, so she checked again – and again it was exactly as it was when she had looked previously. There was nothing out of place.

On the night of the first official investigation, when Brian and Giselle went to the house, the only people there were Andrew and Stacey. It had been decided that they felt it would be best to just walk in and start. In the hall they started to film. Brian said at the very moment the camera was turned on, a ball of light – which was the size of a golf ball and very bright blue – came through the front door. He said that he knew it wasn't the glare from his camera lens. As it came up the hallway it shot between Brian and Andrew. Stacey was screaming and Brian said, "Don't look – just don't look." The light carried on past them and carried on up the hall where it turned a corner and went into a spare room.

Brian followed it, filming the whole time. When he reviewed the tape he told me he had actually caught more than 30 light anomalies. He knows what dust and bugs look like and he said it wasn't anything like that. They stood awestruck as one light came to a table and chairs and, with definite purpose, started to circle them. Brian said that they were standing looking at all the lights around them and he started counting them. When he had got into the 20's he thought, "What the hell is going on?" He had never seen anything like it in all the years he had been investigating. He said to the others, "We are definitely onto something here. This is *really* strange!" At this point he put his K2 meter on the table with his cameras and the light show he caught went on solidly for a couple of hours. They went upstairs and it was exactly the same, there were light anomalies everywhere! Brian says he saw balls of light come out of a room and shoot around the corner and into another room. He admits that at that stage he was stunned by the events he was witnessing.

Then Brian asked if he could see the cupboard with the door that wouldn't stay closed. It was in the bedroom and was facing you as you entered the room. Within minutes, balls of light – some the size of tennis balls – started to come out through the door and into the room, even though the cupboard door was closed at the time. The lights went down the upstairs hallway, down the stairs and out the front door. It was obvious by that time that something was definitely going on with the cupboard! Brian felt that this was the point that everything that was happening started from.

At this point Brian said he was going to stand in the cupboard (as you do!) with his camera. He went in and closed the door and was feeling very apprehensive. He stayed there for a few minutes and asked some questions, but nothing much happened. When he left he decided he would leave his camera running in there and put it on the shelf and closed the door. Everyone then went back down as he didn't want anything to contaminate anything he might catch on the cameras picture or on the sound.

After about 20-30 minutes Brian went back upstairs to retrieve his recorder and to listen to any thing he may have caught. He had got a voice! Brian said when he was in the cupboard he had been asking, "Why are you here? How often do you come here?" To this last question was the reply, "Expect us nightly!" Brian said the voice had a slight accent and the answer was very forcefully given; it was in fact quite menacing in the way it was said. Brian thought, "Oh my God! That was pretty straight to the point!" Brian felt it would be the best course of action to get in more help with the case as it was turning out to be so much more than a lost soul who was walking around the house. There were just too many light anomalies and little things going on than he felt he could cope with himself and decided he should get in a fresh pair of eyes; this would also be able to rule out tricks of the light etc. They arranged to go back again on the next night.

Brian took his wife and younger brother with him, and found that exactly the same things were happening as had the previous night. They all had their cameras running and again it was just like a light show. That was when things started to get weirder and weirder.

After looking around in the property for a while the group decided it was time to take a break and they went downstairs to the living room. Brian made sure that everyone had their cameras and equipment turned off and put his K2 meter on the table. He wanted to make sure that there was no interference for the test he was about to do. Brian's brother asked a question and the K2 meter lit up, all lights on. Brian said it had to be one hell of a hit to make it light up like that! It stayed fully lit for some time.

Brian asked, "Who is with us? Who is causing this?" The K2 lit up again. The group decided this might be a good time to do a yes/no session, they said to light the meter up for 'yes' and leave the lights off for 'no'.

They asked, "Are you a male?" – Yes

"Is there more than one of you here?" – Yes

"Are there more than 10 of you here?" – Yes

The response was perfect on every question. There was no doubt that whatever they were communicating with was intelligent. They were amazed, all this while they were on a break! The responses were non-stop. Brian decided to ask more questions.

"Does something have an issue with Stacey?" – Yes

Stacey said that she could only think of one person who it could possibly be. Brian said not to give him any more information yet, and he carried on questioning.

"Is Stacey on the right track?" – Yes

Stacey then gave a little more information about who she thought it may be.

Brian asked "Is that information correct?" – Yes

Whatever it was that was responding to them, it answered every question that was asked. What claimed to be communicating with them was saying that it was Andrew's Grandmother, who supposedly didn't much like Stacey when she was alive. Brian, Giselle and his brother are quite intuitive people and Brian felt that the spirit wanted Stacey to find something. He asked if that was right and again it answered yes.

Brian said, "Is it something in the house?" – Yes

"Is it a piece of jewellery?" – Yes

"Is it necklace or a ring?" The K2 meter lit up with all lights on as soon as a ring was mentioned. Straight away, Stacey went upstairs and came back with a ring. She put it onto the table and the K2 lit up again!

Brian asked Andrew and Stacey why the ring was important if it was given to Andrew? If the grandmother had not been keen on Stacey, then what was the significance? Stacey asked, "What should I do with the ring?" Brian said to his way of thinking it was just symbolic. He then asked,

"Would it help if Stacey gave the ring back?" – No lights went on.

"Should Stacey put it on your grave?" – Again no lights lit up. He then asked,

"Should she keep the ring?" – Yes

Stacey said that she was now terrified of keeping it in the house after that.

"Would it help if I put it on a Bible?" – The K2 lit up

again!

It was about now that Brian began to suspect that something wasn't quite adding up. Why would putting the ring on a Bible make it OK? He also had a suspicion that they were not communicating with who they thought they were. Something just didn't feel right. He advised everyone to be cautious as there were so many orbs that they couldn't be totally sure who they were in contact with. He told them that he had a feeling that the spirit was just playing with them and just telling them what it thought they wanted to hear. He then turned off the K2 meter and said that it may be better if they focused their attention on the cupboard in the bedroom.

When Brian asked Andrew and Stacey if they knew who had owned the house before, Stacey told him that the house had been in a bit of a mess when they saw it and that the people who had lived there were into some pretty weird "shit" too. Brian asked what and was told that they had been messing about with Ouija boards and things like that. Brian thought, "OK, here we go!" He asked if there was anywhere else in the house that didn't feel right. They then said that they had made a bedroom in the attic and that it had a peculiar atmosphere. If anyone stayed overnight in the room, they didn't like the feeling up there and also didn't have a particularly restful night. Off the group went, to check out the attic.

Brian pulled down the hatch and started to climb up. He told me, "Before I got my head fully into the attic a feeling like a heavy static charge hit me. It was so powerful it actually took my breath away."

His brother followed him up but as soon as he stepped into the room he said, "Don't like it. Not interested!" and went back down. Brian said to me that it was hard to explain the feeling that he got when the energy hit him; it was like a static shock. He said, "I thought there was some really heavy shit going on up there."

He walked down to the end of the room and pointed

his camera at the wall. He didn't know why, but he felt he should take some pictures there. Lights immediately started to come through the wall in front of him. "It was just like a scene from the film *Poltergeist*!" he said to me. He then realized he was standing directly above the cupboard in the bedroom downstairs.

He told the others in the group that it was his feeling that this was the place where someone had been playing with something that they shouldn't have. It was also his belief that they had managed to open a doorway or portal and it was still very much open! Shortly after that they decided to bring the night's investigation to a close.

The next time the group went to the house, Brian took his older brother, who also is a sensitive, as he felt he needed a fresh perspective. Brian had not told him any of the details of the previous visits or where the "hot spots" were.

When they got to the house, the first thing Brian's brother did was to go straight upstairs and straight into the bedroom where the cupboard was. At that time all the lights in the room were on and they all stood looking at the cupboard door. A short time later Brian's brother said, "Jesus – it looks just like a walk through! They just pass straight through here and then off out. That is why there are so many lights. It is not even the same lights you are seeing. Every one is different. This is definitely a portal and they are coming through all the time!" Stacey said that they had used it as their bedroom but could never get a decent night's sleep there. The headboard of the bed was against the wall next to the cupboard door. Brian then told his brother about the previous owners using a Ouija board in the attic. They both came to the conclusion that this was definitely something more "naughty" than an average haunting. Something had come through that portal that was pretty bad.

They turned the lights off then and it was totally dark. The whole group just stood looking at the door. Everyone knew that something was bound to happen. It did.

Brian told me he was standing next to another investigator, as he looked he saw a dark figure peep around the door frame and look out at them. Then it pulled back and disappeared. Brian didn't say a word, then he turned to his companion and said, "You saw that didn't you?" The other investigator just nodded; he was too stunned to speak. Brian asked him to relate exactly what he had seen – it was exactly the same as he had seen himself. As they all stood watching, the very same thing happened again! Brian said that was really unbelievable was that the door was actually closed at the time the figure was seen looking around the door jamb. They all stood just watching. It was just after this that Brian's eye got drawn to the wall. He thought, "What the hell am I looking at?" It was so strange it took a second or two to register. The wall looked like a net curtain that you could see through! There was some kind of scene behind the solid wall and you could see movement behind it. What they saw was hardly believable – a lot of people moving around on the other side through the wall! Brian's brother confirmed what the group was seeing when he said, "It looks just like a large group of people just milling around in there."

Brian said, "This shit just doesn't happen! I have done loads of investigations, but I have *never* seen anything like this!" They came to the firm conclusion that this was the exact spot where the spirits were able to come through. Brian told them to actually stand and watch; it was totally surreal. Soon after this event the group decided enough was enough and for that night they brought the investigation to a close. They all felt too stunned to carry on and needed a while to take in everything they had witnessed.

Brian said to me that after that night things in the house got worse and worse; it got to the point where people were actually being touched and they could feel the hands on them. Brian said, "It was creepy! We knew that we had to shut this portal down."

Even when they were not there investigating, things were still happening to Stacey. One night, she told Brian, she was sitting watching the TV and she saw a ball of light come out of the screen. It was the size of a tennis ball. It went across the room, hit the wall and went straight down through the floor. She also told him that she saw them in broad daylight. It was shortly after this that Brian witnessed one for himself. He was there one night and realized that he was seeing a pulsating green ball of light. He wondered what it was he was seeing this time? He was amazed when he saw it shoot straight up and through the ceiling! He told me, "It was like a bullet; it was like a special effect from a film." At this time he felt it was really getting crazy. On the same night he was in the living room and looking out into the hallway. He saw a little red ball of light, like a laser light (but it wasn't); it went down the window, across the window sill, and down the wall. It came out a little way from the wall, it paused – then shot straight down through the floor. The colour was solid red. There was something about this one that made Brian feel very uncomfortable; maybe it was because it was red and red stands for danger. That one, he said, had really creeped him out! It was the way it moved and the slow methodical way it went down the wall. It was just weird! He told me that he had even begun to doubt what he was seeing as real, was he really seeing what he thought he was? "I have seen some crazy stuff, but this was something else entirely. All these lights went on continually, night after night. It didn't matter what time it was that we went there. As soon as someone went into the house, things started happening. You couldn't walk in and not have something happen! It was almost like as soon as the spirits knew someone was in the house, they would put on a light show. Every time, without fail – it was non-stop, on and on." Brian then told me that the weirdest part was yet to come.

Although Brian wasn't aware of it, Andrew and Stacey

had some problems in their marriage at the time and they decided to part. When Andrew left, the activity dropped off dramatically, although it did not stop altogether. There was, however, a significant change. Brian told me that on looking back he felt that the activity must have been around Andrew and somehow directed towards Stacey. He thought that maybe the stress of the marriage break-up could have fuelled the energy that had built up from when the Ouija board had been played with in the attic. Perhaps the stress had been just the catalyst needed to start all the activity?

Brian asked Stacey when had the problem started with the cupboard door, in relation to when her marriage problems had started? It seemed that the activity in house had started to ramp up at the beginning of their breakdown.

Brian said to me, "People might think: OK – so they saw balls of light and people leaning out of cupboard doors; but this went on for weeks! The activity was relentless, the lights, something walking about – all of it was non-stop. The EVP's we got – everything that happened – it was so prolific, it just was one thing after another. As soon as you walked into the house you could feel a heaviness; almost a palpable weight in the atmosphere there."

Brian said that he lost contact with Stacey when he moved away. The activity was still going on when he left. Stacey still lived at the house and refused to move away – she was determined to stay as the time and effort they had put into the house mattered more to her than all the things that had happened to her there.

Brian says that she is a very brave lady to stay there as the intensity of what went on was more like something from a film – not something that happens in real life! The portal is still open as Stacey says that if she got someone in to close it and it wasn't done right, it may cause more problems for her. She can live with the activity as it is now.

Stacey has also heard on the grapevine that the house next door to her also has problems too. She is not going to get involved with that; she said that she had asked the other owner and in no uncertain terms got told to mind her own business! However, she did find out that in the neighbour's house, the kid's bedroom backed directly on to the wall and cupboard in her own house. She had also heard that there may be 3 or 4 other house in the direct vicinity that may also have problems too.

Brian has put the occurrences in the house down to the fact that someone was messing about with a Ouija board. He says, "A Ouija board is just a board with writing on it. The problem comes with the intent of the user. When we open a communication with spirits and do a session – we make sure to close down properly. We make sure they know and understand that the line of communication is closing down. So, my advice is: if you use Ouija boards and don't know what you are doing – LEAVE THEM WELL ALONE! You never know what you are letting in – and they may decide to stay!"

I have a couple of stories here from Sallie Pollard who lives in Essex in the UK. She and her husband have started to investigate with Spirit Team and they are not disappointed with the investigations they have been on so far. This next story was personal to her and she says:

I would like to tell you what happened to me in a house in Clacton-on-Sea in Essex where I used to live. It all started when I was about 13 (rather clichéd, I know! but that is how it happened). I was sitting on my bed doing my home-work. By the side of my bed is the dressing table with a big mirror where I put my deodorants and things, when I noticed something move out of the corner of my eye. When I turned and looked at my table I saw a bottle (it was a face wash), rise up into the air, move to the left – still in the air, then drop suddenly to the floor!

As soon as I felt brave enough to move and accept what I had just seen, I ran out of my bedroom and told my mum who was in the kitchen. I now believe things had happened to my mum as she told me, "Things happen in this world that we will never understand," instead of the usual, "Stop being silly!" She still to this day won't talk about what happened.

After that day, my wardrobe door – which was one of those built into the wall – kept opening by itself, plus the bedroom door kept opening as well! I saw the doors open in front of me countless times. We had really cold spots where I could see my breath even though the heating was on full blast, and also had spots where there was a really bad smell that would move around my bedroom.

After a few months I talked to a friend's grandmother,

who believed in the supernatural, and she advised me to block all the windows and doors in my bedroom and light a candle in the middle of the room. If there was a spirit the candle would blow out; if there wasn't the candle would burn itself out. I don't know where she got this idea from, but by this time I was so scared I wanted someone to see what was happening to me as my family took no notice of what I said! Well, I did that little experiment – I sat there with my watch and it took precisely 6 minutes 47 seconds for the candle to blow out. Straight after, I did ask to move to another bedroom but my parents said no.

Things carried on and on and I ended up confiding in my friends at school; I think by then I must have been about 14. They said they wanted to stay overnight so I could show them what was happening. Well – nobody stayed overnight! We all saw a book fly off my bookcase and the pages just flapping over by themselves. The last straw was when my best friend got pushed down on the bed and, no matter how hard we tried, we couldn't get her up for about 5 minutes! She never came around to the house again.

I then thought: maybe whoever is doing this wants help. So I went to the library and looked into the building that was there before the house was built. It turned out that there used to be a factory making pianos and there was an accident where a piano fell on top of a woman and killed her. I don't know to this day if it is this woman's spirit who is responsible, but it seems to add up to me. After telling my mum what had been happening for over a year, she moved me into another bedroom and my sister went into my old room. The doors kept opening and closing still, and with her in it. I remember her shouting in the hallway that whoever kept opening the door had better stop it, as it was driving her nuts! A few things happened in my new room but not half as much as in my old bedroom, which I could deal with until I moved out. I do wonder to this day if the poltergeist activity still happens there.

Since that experience it has driven me to find out what exactly could do this kind of thing, and I am now starting to investigate with my husband and we want to show people out there that these things do happen.

Sallie also told me another story about when she had been in contact with a spirit called Anne who she came across while doing an investigation about a year ago at the Colchester Town Hall:

I did contact Anne there and told her I was very sorry about what had happened to her. When I got home my dog (who always goes crazy and very excited whenever I get home) ran away from me and wouldn't go near me for about ten minutes – strange – but I thought nothing of it.

After that we did a spirit box session at home and my husband spoke to a family member called Steve who passed away 15 years ago. We heard Anne talk to him like she was showing him what to do, and after that he came through loud and clear! He carried on talking to Anne until we helped Steve get his message across to his daughters. Since then we have heard nothing at all from him, so we assume he has safely moved on.

I do feel it when Anne is around me; she isn't here all the time but if I think of her then she comes, plus I feel she also talks to me when I sleep, which may sound weird but they are not normal dreams and are very vivid. She has appeared on a camcorder during the day as an orb. It is a nice feeling to know she is with me on investigations. We heard her speak to another spirit at home one Sunday; it was a man and he kept saying at first, "Help me," then we heard Anne saying, "Please leave – now," then after about three minutes she said to him very politely, "I am very sorry but you have to leave this family." We caught all of this on a recorder and I was astonished as I had always believed that a positive spirit can become protective and that they aren't all bad. I don't believe we are haunted at all as she never stays but comes to visit occasionally. One thing I do wonder was how she knew another spirit was with us?

There are a lot of things we don't understand and I think we know only the tip of the iceberg, but with the new technology I believe we will be able to prove scientifically that death is only the beginning.

I have another story here for you, from Wally T. He has asked that his friend not be known by her real name, so for this story we shall call her Mary. He is part of the NPT Force team of investigators in Nevada.

I told my friend Mary about astral projection; I was very interested in it at the time and she thought it sounded interesting. I had her lay on the bed and was telling her what she needed to do. After 5 – 10 minutes I felt terrified. I didn't really know what was bothering me. However I had been using a Ouija board earlier that night, so I put it in the hall out of the way.

I was feeling afraid for Mary – I was staring at my friend lying on the bed. After a minute or so everything went dark and I couldn't see. Suddenly – I could see again. Mary had a grey metallic sphere on her stomach. I had this feeling that she WAS the sphere! Then I felt something else in the room. I looked around the room to see what if anything else was there. I saw the outline of "something" run across the room to be next to Mary, it looked to be about 3-4 feet tall and was dark, like it was made out of shadow. It was yanking at the sphere. Suddenly I could no longer see it.

When Mary "woke up", she told me she felt if she opened her eyes that she would have been able to see herself. She could almost feel her nose touching her own nose – she also felt two presences in the room. One she couldn't tell anything about, but the other seemed to be friendly; she said the friendly one disappeared for a moment. She told me she could feel something tug at her while she was on the bed. I had not touched her in any way and she told me all of this before I told her anything about what I had seen!

Well, here is a very spooky one! It was sent in to me from Jose Amesquita 2nd. He is a member of Historical Paranormal and they are from Ohio. I'm very pleased I didn't see it! He says:

My first ghost encounter happened when I was five years old. My aunt Maggie had passed away a week prior. I was so hurt. She was my first relative that I had known who had passed away and we had been very close. At the time of her passing it was hard to cope.

Now the bed I loved to sleep in was a pull-out from the couch. At night all the lights in the house would be out except the one in the kitchen. Where my bed was, you could see into the kitchen. I wasn't sleeping very well and I opened my eyes slowly, and when I did – I saw a black figure standing at the bottom of the bed facing me! The kitchen light was so bright I should have been able to see who the person was – but it was pure black! But I did recognize who it was – it was Aunt Maggie.

I actually smiled at her, but as soon as I did – horns grew from the head of the thing! I instantly stopped smiling. I was frozen; I couldn't breathe or move. I tried screaming for my parents – but nothing came out! All I could do was close my eyes (I'm starting to tear up because I was SO scared!). Every time I opened my eyes it was still there. Finally, after what seemed like an eternity, I was able to scream – and the demon disappeared!

Ever since that day I have been able to see and feel spirits. I would have encounters often and still do to this day. That is why I am in a paranormal group – to try and find answers to the other side.

AFTERWORD

Well, reader, I hope that you enjoyed all the stories you found here. I have to say that I thank from the bottom of my heart all those people who I found on Twitter for providing me – and you – with some very interesting stories.

What I have found while compiling this is that, although many people have had things that have happened, quite a few are still reluctant to speak about them. As you have read – I had no such worries! Perhaps by reading this you may realise it is not that unusual, as many of these stories came from people who are not affiliated to paranormal groups, but are just Joe Public, like me. Tell people your story if you have one; you might just be surprised at the reception it gets. There are more believers out there than you may think.

Again, so many thanks go to those people I have cajoled, shamed, pushed and prodded in getting these stories for you; I couldn't have done it without you all. I should also say that, unless you keep sending them in, this will probably be the only one!

If you do have a story or two you may want to share, contact me at the following email address and we shall see what we can do – gammonsghosts@gmail.com.

ACKNOWLEDGEMENTS

WARREN COATES	NORTHERN IRELAND PARANORMAL RESEARCH ASSOC – N.I.P.R.A.
KIM GOOD	CONCORDE ANTIOCH PARANORMAL SOCIETY – C.A.P.S.
CHRIS P	TEXAS
TOBY OWENBY	USA
MARK VERNON	WAKEFIELD, YORKSHIRE, ENGLAND
	markbeezneez@gmail.com
TONY PARKES	SOUTH DEVON, ENGLAND
JOSE AMESQUITA 2nd	HISTORICAL PARANORMAL INVESTIGATORS, OREGON, U.S.A
BRENDA NEWBY	SPIRIT RESEARCH TEAM – DALLAS, TEXAS
SALLIE POLLARD	ESSEX, ENGLAND

BRIAN HOLLOWAY	GIBRALTAR, PARANORMAL TV SHOW CO HOST
MIKE BAGOZZI	THPI – GREENBAY, U.S.A
WALLY T.	NEVADA PARANORMAL TASK FORCE www.nevadaparanormaltaskforce.com
GARY TAYLOR	PRIVATE PARANORMAL INVESTIGATOR, ENGLAND
CHRISTINE DONNELLY	HIDDEN REALMS PARANORMAL, ENGLAND www.hiddenrealms.org.uk
DENNIS HEMMINGS	HIDDEN REALMS PARANORMAL, ENGLAND
NOE OLIVER	PRIVATE PARANORMAL INVESTIGATOR, U.S.A
HECTOR BARRAGAN Jnr	FOUNDER OF SOUTHERN ARIZONA GHOST & PARA. SOC

STEPHANIE CARPENTER	PACT PARANORMAL, NORTH CAROLINA U.S.A
	www.pactparanormalinvestigations.yolasite.com
	www.facebook.com/pactparanormal
JEREMY STARK	FOUNDER OF TRUE HUNTING PARANORMAL INVESTIGATIONS, WISCONSIN U.S.A
CULZ PARANORMAL	culzparanormalinvestigators.webs.com

BOOKS BY JAN MCDONALD

If you also like fictional paranormal investigations, then I strongly suggest that you check out these books by Jan McDonald:

Mike Travis Paranormal Investigations
The Crowsmoor Curse: getBook.at/Crowsmoorcurse

Long Shadows: getBook.at/longshadows

The Sacred Ark: getBook.at/sacredark

The Haunted Diary of Victoria Little: getBook.at/haunteddiary

The Merlin Manuscript: getBook.at/merlin

The Sin Eater: getbook.at/sineater

Mike Travis short stories
Beginnings: getBook.at/Beginnings

Halloween: getBook.at/halloween

Christmas Spirits: getBook.at/christmasspirits

The Beckett Vampire Trilogy
Midnight Wine: getBook.at/midnightwine

Lycan: getBook.at/lycan

Part 3 coming 2015

www.ingramcontent.com/pod-product-compliance
Lightning Source LLC
LaVergne TN
LVHW051607070426
835507LV00021B/2824